DEALING with the STUFF that makes LIFE tough

The 10 THINGS That Stress GIRLS Out and HOW to COPE with Them

Jill Zimmerman Rutledge, M.S.W., LCSW

Contemporary Books

Chicago   New York   San Francisco   Lisbon   London   Madrid   Mexico City
Milan   New Delhi   San Juan   Seoul   Singapore   Sydney   Toronto

Library of Congress Cataloging-in-Publication Data

Rutledge, Jill Zimmerman.
  Dealing with the stuff that makes life tough / Jill Zimmerman Rutledge.
      p.   cm.
    ISBN 0-07-142326-5 (acid-free paper)
      1. Teenage girls—Psychology.   2. Young women—Psychology.
  3. Identity (Psychology).   4. Self-acceptance.   5. Stress
  management.   6. Self-confidence.
  7. Adjustment (Psychology).   I. Title.

  HQ798.R88 2004
  305.235—dc21   2003046047

This book is dedicated to the memory of
Sue Kramer and
Doris and Norman Hefter

1 2 3 4 5 6 7 8 9 0   AGM/AGM   2 1 0 9 8 7 6 5 4 3

ISBN 0-07-142326-5

Interior design by Susan H. Hartman

This book is printed on acid-free paper.

Contents

Acknowledgments   v

Introduction
From Me to You   vii

1 *"If Everyone Says I Look Fine,*
Why Do I Feel So Fat?"
Making Peace with Body Image   1

2 *High Anxiety*
Panic Attacks and Other
Frightening Fears   25

3 *The Sun Through the Clouds*
When You Feel Down   51

4 *Venus to Mars*
Dealing with Guys   73

5 *Not "Just Saying 'No'"*
Smoking, Drinking, Drugs   91

6 *Fresh Air*
Taking Back Your Overscheduled Life   113

7 *Picking up the Pieces*
When Your Parents' Divorce
Shatters Life as You Know It   137

8 *Mr. Sandman, Bring Me a Dream*
Getting to Sleep When You Can't   163

9 *Enough Already!*
Bullies and So-Called Friends   179

10 *When Your Crush Is a Girl*
Lesbian Teens   195

Afterword
Landing on Your Feet   213

Resources for Your Journey   215

Acknowledgments

I would like to thank Judith Barnard; Neela Bindu; Louise Pappageorge; my agent, Susan Cohen, and her assistant, Rebecca Sherman; my editor, Michele Pezzuti, Nancy Hall, Cori Moriarty, and everyone else at Contemporary Books; Andrew Rutledge; Daniel Rutledge; Jonathan Rutledge; and, most of all, Bob.

Introduction

From Me to You

ear Reader,

The Wizard of Oz is one of my favorite stories of all time. On the surface, it's a fantasy about a little girl, Dorothy, and her dog, Toto, who are lost in the Land of Oz. They meet friends—the Tin Man, the Scarecrow, and the Cowardly Lion. They have adventures. They kill evil witches. They meet a good witch and a wizard who help them find their way back to their warm, safe, comfortable home in Kansas.

But like any good story, it has a deeper meaning. Dorothy and her friends go to the Wizard with the naïve, childlike hope that he will have magical solutions to their problems. Yet the Wizard's "magic" is simply a new perspective: he enables them to see that they *already* possess the inner power to solve their own problems.

Most everyone knows the story. The Tin Man asks the Wizard to give him a "heart." He learns that he actually *is* a very kind, compassionate, loving person. The Scarecrow asks for "brains." He learns that he *already* has intelligence—he just needs to believe in himself. The Cowardly Lion asks for "courage." He learns that he in fact *is* fearless. And Dorothy, who asks the Wizard to send her back to Kansas, learns that she possesses the means to do this for herself. On her feet are ruby slippers, which need only a few clicks before she hears her aunt's soothing voice in her very own bedroom.

So much can be learned from Dorothy's story. It is a story of empowerment—a feeling of inner strength and goodness. It is a story of self-discovery. Dorothy's ruby slippers gave her all the power she needed to cope with her situation. But she had to learn what they were and how she could use them to her advantage. Had Dorothy known that she could simply click her heels three times and be home in a split second, how much calmer and more confident she would have felt when strange, stressful—and sometimes terrifying—experiences crossed her path on her way to meet the Wizard.

Like Dorothy and her friends, we all have certain strengths to help us cope with difficulties. We have skills to soothe ourselves when we feel emotionally overloaded. We all have ruby slippers, the power to calm down and rise above the storm of stress that life can bring. We just have to find them!

I wrote this book for any girl who wants to discover ways to feel calmer inside and cope with her life's ups and downs better. We learn a lot of things in school. But we usually don't learn how to deal with life's frustrations and difficult situations *ourselves*. As girls, our culture teaches us to value our emotional, caring qualities. We learn how to take care of others, but we don't often learn how to care for *ourselves*. We don't learn how to calm our emotions so that we can think things through clearly. We don't learn that we have strengths *inside* ourselves and resources *outside* ourselves to deal with just about anything. If we're lucky, we have adult female role models who teach us how to deal with stress. But too many times, adults can't calm down either!

Finding ways to calm down is important to your physical *and* emotional health. Research shows that too much stress can cause your immune system to become depressed, which means you're more likely to get sick when you can't cope with stress. And calming-down skills will help you cope with your *emotions*, no matter how painful or confusing they may be.

This book will show you lots of ways to calm down. In each chapter, you'll find stories about how three girls coped with a particular problem. I've used true-life stories that my patients have told me throughout the years, although names and identifying information have been changed.

You don't have to read this book cover to cover. Pick and choose chapters, depending on your mood or your situation. Read about calming skills that other girls have used successfully and then try some yourself. See which ones work for you too. And even if you're not *personally* struggling with the issue in a specific chapter, you might know a friend who is. Reading through all the chapters can help you gain a better understanding of what your friend is experiencing and give you some ideas about how to help her.

Remember this: there's no such thing as a stress-free life. No matter who you are, what color your skin is, how much money your parents make (or don't make), how old you are, what kind of grades you get, where you live, where you shop, what you look like—we are all Dorothys trying to get back home to a peaceful feeling inside. *Everyone* needs to find her own ruby slippers, her own power to calm down and cope.

Finding *your* ruby slippers will give you a sense of well-being. You'll feel more centered. You'll feel more in control. You'll feel more confident. You will deal with stress better because you will feel better from the inside out.

You could be part of the most empowered generation of girls and young women the world has ever known! Knowledge is power, and when you know how to calm yourself down, you have an inner power that no one can take away!

I hope you will be inspired to make a list of your own special ways to calm down and cope. And add to it forever!

Please write and let me know how this book works for you. I would truly appreciate your comments and suggestions.

Love,

Jill

E-mail: jszrer1981@aol.com

Website: jillzimmermanrutledge.com

"If Everyone Says I Look Fine, Why Do I Feel So Fat?"

Making Peace with Body Image

*B*ody image. Does any other issue create more turmoil inside the hearts and minds of women and girls? When we were babies, we loved our bodies. We kicked our legs and patted our tummies. We were so pleased with our bodies.

So many of us have lost the little girl who loved her body. Instead, we make long lists of our bodies' downfalls. How many of us wish our butts were smaller, our stomachs were flatter, or that we could be taller or shorter? How many of us wish that we had bigger or smaller breasts or more "definition" in our muscles? When you have poor body image, you can feel trapped on an endless superhighway in your mind. Signs and signals like "I'm ugly" or "I'm too fat" race on with overwhelming speed—and you don't see any exits.

Some people define *body image* as how we think and feel about our bodies, but that's only part of it. Body image is also created by what we think and feel about *ourselves*, how we behave, who we choose for friends, and the culture we live in. If you feel bad about yourself, you probably feel bad about your body too. Or if all your friends are dieting, you may begin to think *you* need to lose weight too.

You may dislike your body for lots of other reasons. For one thing, magazines and other media can have a negative impact on your body image. When we look at pictures of very thin models, many of us want to lose weight immediately so we can look like them. You may also be dissatisfied with your body because of the normal "bloat" you get around your period. Bad moods, being teased about being fat, and weight gain are other reasons you may feel bad about your body.

In the late 1990s, Dr. David Gardner, a well-known researcher on body image, did a survey of more than three thousand women, from ages 13 to 90. He found that more than 62 percent of women between 13 and 19 felt dissatisfied with their bodies. Dr. Gardner also found that the majority of women— 89 percent!—wanted to lose weight. One more startling statistic: 24 percent of women said that they'd sacrifice more than three years of their lives to be at the weight they wanted.

Feeling bad about our bodies interferes with our lives. Your poor body image may make you feel awkward and self-conscious with guys. As 16-year-old Tina put it, "No guy wants a fat girl, and I'm fat. I know if I start liking a guy, I'll just get rejected so why bother?" You may feel so uncomfortable about your body that you go to the beach in long shorts and a baggy T-shirt, instead of a bathing suit. You may be so fearful about gaining weight that you never want to get pregnant.

When you feel dissatisfied with your body, it's important to look at your life as a whole. What else could you be unhappy about? Do you have low self-esteem? Do you exercise moderately but regularly? (Moderate—not obsessive—exercise helps you develop positive feelings about your body.) Are you having problems with family or friends? Are you eating healthily or loading up on junk food? Poor body image feels like it has everything to do with your body but in fact, it also has to do with how you're coping with your life.

As actress Jamie Lee Curtis put it, "I'm not saying that I don't exercise or that I don't suck in my stomach. But I won't go on an insane diet or go to the gym for four hours to change what nature intended. The biggest lesson is that nothing on the exterior will make me feel better. It may seem that way for a short time, but those feelings of inadequacy will [re]surface."

Do you have a poor body image? Take this short quiz to see.

1. How do you feel about how you look?
    a. Very good
    b. OK
    (c.) Mixed feelings
    d. Bad, ashamed

2. Are you happy with your current weight?
    a. Very happy
    b. Happy enough
    (c.) Somewhat unhappy
    d. Very unhappy

3. Have you ever felt too fat after reading an article that reveals the body weight of a model or actress?
    a. Yes
    (b.) No

4. If you gained five pounds, you'd
    a. Be OK with that—five pounds isn't a big deal
    b. Feel neutral—not good or bad
    c. Feel somewhat unhappy
    (d.) Feel very upset

5. When someone says you look nice, you think:
    a. I'm looking good.
    b. They don't have anything else to say.
    (c.) They're trying to make me feel good.
    d. They're lying—they really think I'm gross.

Scoring: For questions 1, 2, 4, and 5, give yourself 1 point for a, 2 points for b, 3 points for c, and 4 points for d. For question 3, give yourself 1 point for a and 2 points for b. If you have a total score of 5–9, you're on the road to a good body image. Keep it up! If you scored 10–15, you may have some body image issues to work out. If you scored more than 16, you may have a poor body image.

Here are the stories of three girls who are learning to make peace with their bodies. Read this chapter and get some ideas on how you too can feel better about how you look. Get on the road to better body image! It's your birthright!

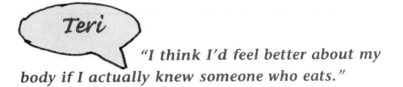

"I think I'd feel better about my body if I actually knew someone who eats."

Teri is 14, short, talkative, and smart. By anyone's standards, she looks like a healthy, normal, attractive girl. By anyone's standards—except hers, that is.

I know it sounds weird, but I think I'm soooo fat. I was a pudgy little kid—I guess I don't think I ever lost my "baby fat," like all my friends. Everyone I know is skinny except for me. I grew four inches last summer, but I also gained 14 pounds. So instead of getting slimmer, I'm just getting fatter. My doctor says all girls gain weight before they get their periods, but I haven't gotten mine yet so I just think I'm fat for no reason.

Teri's mother is so into health food that she doesn't buy anything with fat in it. She exercises at least an hour a day at the health club, plays tennis three times a week, and runs 50 miles a week. Teri's paternal grandfather died of a heart attack at age 42, so her dad is a health fanatic too.

We have fat-free cookies and crackers, fat-free salad dressing, fat-free ice cream, fat-free every-thing. I am so sick of eating crackers that taste like cardboard. My brother and I get rewarded for eating, say, an apple for dessert. They say things like, "it's so nice to see you choose something healthy." But if we eat a cookie, our parents tell us that we're making "bad food choices." My mom constantly tells me to watch my weight so I don't get a heart attack when I'm her age. She says things like "that brownie will catch up with you at some point." It makes me feel paranoid to eat. I feel like I don't deserve the brownie because I'm fat and ugly.

Teri's friends all skip lunch at school. Last year, in eighth grade, Teri's typical lunch was a sandwich, chips, some grapes, and a cookie. But now she feels like a social reject if she eats, because:

1. Not one of Teri's friends eats and she thinks she's fatter than all of them.
2. Once Teri ate a sandwich and everyone looked at her and talked about how much she was eating.
3. The boys tease girls who eat lunch.

Teri's poor body image was partly due to the pressure she felt from friends and family to ignore her natural appetite. To please her parents and to fit in socially, she set up a pattern of starving during the day, which led to binge eating at night. (This is a common pattern among starvers. When nourishment is lacking, the body tries to get as much of it as possible when food is available. It's as if your body is telling you, "Take care of me! I need energy, and food is energy! Make up for skipped meals! Eat!") This behavior only made Teri feel worse about her body—and bad about herself as a person.

I feel like it's impossible to eat like a "normal" person. If I'm hungry during the day, I don't eat because I don't want to be the only one. Then I get home and I'm starving so I eat a lot of fruit. That leads to me sneaking graham crackers and ice cream. I get disgusted with myself for eating so much. Sometimes I skip dinner because I feel so gross, but then I get hungry late at night and stuff myself again, in secret, in my room. It's a vicious circle, because I can't stop thinking about how fat I am, but

*I have so much trouble controlling my appetite. This
definitely makes me feel like shit.*

Teri's mom took her to a nutritionist. Teri learned
that to feel better about herself and her body, she *had*
to learn to eat regular, balanced, healthy meals. The
two reasons for this are:

1. **When you eat regular, balanced, healthy meals,
   you get your metabolism back on track.** Starving and bingeing slows down your metabolism;
   eating well actually speeds it up. When our metabolism's on track, we can learn to trust our bodies.
   We feel better about ourselves because we can eat
   normally and still be in great shape. (This may
   sound paradoxical, but it's absolutely true.)
2. **Balanced meals mean balanced body chemistry.** Your body chemistry—blood sugar, elec-
   trolytes (body salts like calcium and potassium),
   protein levels, and so on—affects your moods.
   And when you're in a bad mood, you're more
   likely to feel bad about your body. We need to give
   our bodies appropriate amounts of proteins, carbohydrates, fats, and water to help ourselves to
   feel better from the inside out.

*My nutritionist showed me a graph about what
happens to your body's blood-sugar level when you
don't eat. That was really interesting. I had no idea
that I was doing anything wrong to my body, but the
graph showed me that the reason I'm starving when I*

get home from school is because I don't eat anything all day, and my blood sugar is at its lowest. I want to be vegetarian, and my nutritionist said I could but I had to do it right.

But understanding that you need to eat well and actually doing it are two different things. The former is easy; the latter is hard. Here's how Teri learned how to get her eating—and body image—back to healthy.

Lunch Goal: Starting with a Sandwich

Teri knew it was important to start eating lunch at school, but she was scared. Her nutritionist helped her develop a strategy to ease into lunch—slowly.

First, Teri did a lunch-eating experiment. For two weeks, she put a cheese sandwich and an apple in her backpack and ate them for lunch. It was tolerable for her to eat the apple in the lunchroom—some of the other girls ate one piece of fruit for lunch so she didn't feel so weird. She ate the cheese sandwich in the library. The important thing was that she was adding calcium, protein, and carbohydrates—three much needed items—to her meal plan. Plus, eating lunch raised her blood-sugar level, which made her feel less hungry later in the day. This helped her after-school bingeing problem immensely.

The conclusion to her experiment was that she did not gain weight, even though she ate a little lunch at school. These results made her feel more confident and positive about her body.

At first I didn't believe that eating something at school would help at all. I thought I'd just get upset and feel even fatter. But I found out that it did help. It was sort of weird—I didn't feel so frantic for food after school. Plus, as long as no one saw me eat anything but an apple I felt OK. It's sad that my school's like that—like girls don't eat, but that's how it is. Well, it was amazing to me that I didn't gain weight, but I didn't. Now I've added chips, a yogurt, and sometimes a cookie. And I've started eating oatmeal or a muffin for breakfast too. And I eat some fat—that one's hard but my nutritionist said some fats are good for you, like olive oil and peanut butter. So my mom is wrong about that. I think I have a little more energy. I used to practically fall asleep in school, but I don't do that anymore.

Taking Some Action: A *Moderate* Exercise Plan

Teri began a simple, moderate exercise program. On weekends and once or twice after school, she walks or jogs for 30 minutes. Also, her neighbor is a personal trainer at the local YMCA, and he showed her how to work out with light weights. Teri does this twice a week. In a few weeks she felt stronger, which helped improve her body image.

Exercise helps me feel better about my body. My mom obsesses about exercise but I try not to because that just makes me feel bad about myself all over again. I try not to get mad at myself for skipping a day of jogging because I have a cold and don't feel like it. I just think about the next day or the day after that, when I'll be able to exercise again. I feel like if I exercise two or three times a week, that's fine. My mom has to exercise every day for like an hour. It's crazy.

Magazine Overload Antidote: Teri's Good Body Image Scrapbook

Pictures of perfect models and perfect actresses drive Teri crazy. She always compares herself to them and feels ugly. So she had the idea to make a good body image scrapbook.

This is how. Teri cut pictures out of magazines of healthy-looking women. Then she got some pieces of colored construction paper (you can get this at an art store, a drugstore, or a supermarket), punched three holes down the left side of each one, and pasted on the pictures—one on each piece of paper. She tied the pages together with a piece of yarn that she weaved through the holes and tied with a bow. That way, she can add pictures easily—she just unties the bow of yarn and then ties on new pages.

When she feels fat, Teri looks through her scrapbook. It gives her a different, more positive perspective on what's considered "attractive."

I got this idea from a friend who makes scrapbooks as birthday presents. My scrapbook was a birthday present to myself! My friend buys these expensive blank books for scrapbooks, but my way is much cheaper and I think more creative. I have pictures of healthy, normal people, like Jennifer Lopez, Kate Winslet, Drew Barrymore, and Oprah Winfrey. I also have pictures of athletes like Mia Hamm and the WNBA players. They look so cool, and they're not skinny. If any of them gets skinny, I'll just rip their picture out! Actually, I went through some magazines and threw away pictures of the skinniest girls. Right in the garbage.

I definitely think that my body image is changing a little—I used to think Calista Flockhart was perfect, but now I think she looks like an underfed mouse. She's sick looking to me now. I'm eating healthier and I have more energy. It's hard, but I'm beginning to think my body could be fine just the way it is. At least I'm thinking that it's a possibility. That's an improvement for me.

Jenny

"It all started with a comment from my doctor's nurse."

Jenny is 13 and already 5 feet 8 inches tall. Ever since kindergarten she's been the tallest person in her class, which has made her self-conscious about her body for years. But after her eighth-grade checkup, she felt like she was the fattest one in the class too.

I'll never forget this as long as I live. I was so humiliated. I was at the doctor's for my eighth-grade physical, and the nurse weighed me. I still remember what she looked like: Petite, about five inches shorter than me, and wearing a white dress. I remember she had a really flat stomach. She looked at the numbers on the scale and said, "Oh, you're OK now, but don't gain any more weight, ever. You'll thank me when you're 40."

I was mortified. I only weighed 140 pounds and I thought I was fine. But after that comment, for the first time, I felt like the fattest blimp in the world. I felt like I should wear a coat all day in school so no one could see how fat I was. I thought that's what the nurse was saying to me—that I'm fat and ugly and I need to lose weight.

Later that day, Jenny asked her mom what she thought. Her mom was supportive and told Jenny not to worry about her weight, but that didn't help Jenny's feelings at all. The nurse's thoughtless, insensitive, and stupid comment made Jenny feel more miserable and insecure than she had ever felt before.

I tried not to think about it because I was scared I'd get an eating disorder or something. But I couldn't get the words out of my head—"don't gain any more weight, ever." I couldn't concentrate on my schoolwork for a week. I cried in my room, I was just so upset.

Jenny didn't know what to do. Talking to her mom didn't really help ("She's my *mom*. What's she going to say? That I am fat? I don't think so!") Then she thought of her aunt, who's a social worker. Aunt Sally had been bulimic when she was a teenager, but she's been recovered for 20 years and now she counsels girls with eating disorders. Jenny had always felt close to her.

I called Aunt Sally. She was great. She told me the nurse should lose her license for saying that to me. I thought that was cool—I felt like she understood how much pain that nurse inflicted on me. My aunt gave me some different ways to think about the whole situation. I felt a lot better.

Here are Aunt Sally's words of wisdom.

- **Aunt Sally told Jenny that feeling fat when you're not is called a *distorted feeling*.** Another word for distorted is *twisted*. Distorted, twisted feelings are not the real world. They're just feelings and they can't hurt you if you don't let them. Talk to yourself! Tell your distorted feelings to shut up. Tell them they aren't real. Say it out loud! (In Jenny's case, she told the stupid nurse to shut up too. One day in her bedroom she shouted, "Shut up, you moron!" And she felt great!)

- **Aunt Sally told Jenny that it's *normal* and *necessary* for a girl to gain weight during puberty.** Your body needs fat to produce hormones so you'll get regular menstrual periods—and the nurse was way out of line, and medically misinformed, when she told Jenny not to "gain any more weight, ever."

- **Aunt Sally told Jenny to treat herself like she treats her best friend.** So Jenny thought, "If my best friend gained weight, would I hate her?" Of course the answer was, "No—she'd still be my best friend." Then Aunt Sally and Jenny had a conversation about the fact that Jenny could—and should—support herself like she supports her friends. If she would still like a friend who had gained weight, shouldn't she still like herself—no matter what the scale read? "After I thought about this, I knew my aunt was right. I was being too hard on myself. I do that a lot."

- **Aunt Sally explained that the nurse was *projecting her feelings* onto Jenny.** Secure, confident people don't judge others. They have no need to make people feel bad. On the contrary, they try to help people feel good and successful. The nurse was insecure about *herself.* She was most likely anxious about her own weight and misplaced her feelings—she expressed anxiety about *Jenny's* weight. This is called *projection*, which some people do when they feel bad about themselves—they project their problems onto other people.

The information about projection helped Jenny see the nurse as weak, insecure, and, well . . . pathetic. Jenny suddenly had a new perspective.

I mean, you can't respect the comments of a pathetic person. Sometimes it's hard and I hear her words, but I'm not going to let this nurse control how I feel about my body. It's hard enough to like your body. Her comments are like pollution, and I don't need her polluting my body image. Sometimes when her words enter my mind, I imagine that I put them in the trash and delete them, like on a computer.

Aunt Sally recommended a cool book, *Body Traps* by Dr. Judith Rodin. "I like this book because it has all sorts of self tests, like the self-nurturance test and the emotional eating test. It helps me to think about why I'm so afraid of getting fat. I realized that it wasn't just the nurse's comment. I wouldn't have reacted so badly if I felt good about my body in the first place."

Jenny learned other ways to help her feel better about her body.

A Flower a Week

Jenny loves fresh flowers. They remind her that nature is diverse—trees and flowers aren't all the same. They also remind her that we can think of our bodies as not having to be all the same, too. Somehow this thought helps and reassures Jenny as she tries to develop a more positive body image.

So I buy myself a flower on Saturdays. A different kind of flower every week. I put it in a little vase in my room, and when I look at it, I think that it's beautiful. It reminds me that I can like my body the way it is. I'm trying to choose to do that instead of feeling too fat all the time.

Baby Pictures

When Jenny looks at her baby pictures, she appreciates that she wasn't born into this world with a poor body image. And that she can get back to liking her body again, like she did when she was little.

I asked my mom if I could see my baby book. There were all these pictures of me laughing and looking happy. I was a cute baby. My body looked just right. I framed a few pictures and put them on my dresser. When I look at myself as a baby, I think, "Yes! I deserve to feel good about my body again, like I did then!"

Amy

"I wish my mother and my sisters weren't so skinny. I'm sort of fat, and they make me feel even fatter, like humongous."

Amy is 15. She's the middle child, in between two sisters. She wants to be a journalist someday—and write about girls and body image.

Amy is a lot heavier than her sisters. She takes after her father—she has a short, stocky build. Her sisters both look like their mother—tall and slender. Amy's mother is naturally thin. She doesn't diet or exercise and hasn't gained a pound since high school. Amy, on the other hand, feels she gains weight just *looking* at food. Amy's mother doesn't understand why Amy feels bad about her body. She thinks that if Amy wants to be slim, she just has to accept her "genes" and eat less. This makes Amy feel sad and resentful—and guilty.

My mom means well, but all she does is tell me what not to eat. "Don't eat that cake. Don't eat that cookie." She'll bake chocolate chip cookies for the family and then tell me not to eat one! She says I don't "need" it. I get the feeling that she's embarrassed to have me as a daughter because I'm not thin like her. She says that's not true, but I think it is. She makes me think it's all my fault.

Amy saw her pediatrician for a checkup and they had a conversation about her weight. It went pretty well. Amy's doctor made four important points:

1. She's in the high weight range for her age because she's got a larger bone structure than many girls, and she tends to put on weight easily.
2. She'd be healthier if she could lose about 15 or 20 pounds, but she shouldn't try to lose more than that because of her body type.

3. She should try to make better food choices for herself. Her mom shouldn't make them for her.
4. She should get some regular exercise—even taking a 20-minute walk every day would be great.

Amy asked her doctor to tell these things to her mother so she'd understand.

After my doctor explained things to my mom, she definitely backed off about my eating. She doesn't talk much about food to me, and we get along much better. I think I'm making better food choices too. I'm eating more fruit than I used to. I'm walking my dog more. I think I was eating a lot of junk when my mom was after me because I was mad at her. I do want to lose some weight. Kids tease me about being big and I want them to stop. Now I tell myself I can have a cookie or something, but that if I want the whole box I have to wait 10 minutes to eat any more. It's like delayed gratification—if I want more I can have it, but after 10 minutes I usually don't want more.

What the doctor said about my big bones and stuff—well, that made me feel good and bad. Good, because it's not my fault I'm not skinny. It's not because of my willpower exactly. But I also feel bad because all the women in my family are thin except me. Who wants big bones? Who wants to be fat? No girl I know. It's painful.

Here's what helped Amy's body image.

Getting into the Swim

Amy joined an extramural swim club at school—and much to her own amazement, she likes it! Amy also thinks this helps her feel better about her body.

I feel good about the swimming thing. It's not supercompetitive and it's fun. I feel good, swimming the laps. We do that to increase our endurance and at first I was terrible. I could only swim one lap. But I stuck with it and now I'm much better. I feel like my body's getting in shape—you know, toned and stuff. And it makes me feel good. My sisters are very unathletic, and here I have a sport. And I've made some new friends.

Getting a Guy's Perspective

Amy finds comfort in talking to her best guy friend, Jason. Amy's known Jason since second grade and even though they've never been "boyfriend/girlfriend," she feels close to him—like a brother.

I think guys have a perspective that my girlfriends just don't have. I think they are more honest than girls. They just tell you what they think, instead of what they think you want to hear.

Jason told me that he thinks when girls don't eat, they're acting stupid. He thinks they want to be thin for each other, because guys like him (and he's really cool!) aren't turned on by toothpick girls. Jason said he thinks I'm cute, I have a great personality, and that I'm not that fat. He says I'm healthier looking than the skinny girls. That really helps me feel good about myself, even though I'm not thin.

Affirmations

Amy finds that using affirmations helps her stay on the better body image track. Affirmations are positive things you say to yourself to boost your self-esteem and body image. Instead of giving yourself negative messages, like "I'm so fat and ugly," you affirm the *good things* about yourself. You say, "Yes!" to yourself. As you practice using affirmations, you will begin to *feel positive* about yourself too.

When she wakes up in the morning, Amy thinks up an affirmation for the day. She says the affirmation to herself when she's brushing her teeth, and again, just before she goes to sleep at night. During the day, if she finds herself feeling fat, she repeats the affirmation to herself.

Here are some of **Amy's Affirmations**.

- I'm smart and strong and good. I'm learning to love who I am.
- I have many achievements. I am proud of myself for _____ (fill in the blank)
- Healthy eating = Healthy body.
- My body is me. I try to love myself and my body.

- My body is getting fit. My body is fine.
- I take care of my body. My body takes care of me.
- My body works hard. I respect my body and treat it well.
- Today is a new day. I will appreciate my body today.
- Health = Happiness. I will feed myself well.
- I want to live and to be healthy. I need a strong body to live and to be healthy.

Experiment with Amy's Affirmations! Make up your own and have fun!

Summing It Up

Teri, Jenny, and Amy found lots of different ways to deal with their body image problems. Their solutions are only the beginning—ideas to get *your* creative juices flowing.

Are you the sentimental type? Then try making a scrapbook, like Teri, or find your old baby pictures, like Jenny.

Do you crave information? All three girls did, and they found ways to help gain perspective on their body image issues. You might want to meet with a nutritionist, like Teri. You might talk to a trusted friend or family member, like Jenny. Or you might talk to your doctor, like Amy. Books like *Body Traps* can help too—your bookstore or library will have an entire section on body image self-help books. (You can also find them online.) Browse through as many books as you can. See if you can find one that might increase *your* understanding of *your* body image issues.

No Body's Perfect by Kimberly Kirberger is another good book on body image. (These books and more are listed in Resources for Your Journey at the back of the book.)

Are you the social type? Then talk to a guy friend, like Amy—or a girlfriend who's had similar feelings. Friends can support your good body image—and you can support theirs.

Do you need to lose some weight to be healthier? Join a sports class or club, like Amy. Sometimes it's easier—and more motivating—if you have a workout buddy, so try to find one. Research shows that physical activity can help everyone—overweight or not—improve general health and body image. (Just don't push yourself too hard—obsessive exercise isn't good for you—period.) And don't deny your treats. Enjoy them—but use Amy's idea of *delayed gratification* to help you limit the amounts.

Do you starve during the day to lose weight, only to binge at night? Try Teri's lunch-eating experiment. Make a goal to eat something substantial, like a sandwich, for lunch. Eat breakfast too. You'll be surprised how much better you feel and how much more energy you'll have. You may even feel better about your body because you'll see that you *can eat* and be *healthy*. (If you find that you can't break your unhealthy eating habits on your own, talk to your parents about seeing a therapist for some help.)

As Teri says, "I don't want to be like my mom. She's obsessed with her body. I just want to find my own way. I mean, I'm a human being. I want to feel like I deserve to eat. I don't want to be skin and bones. I want to learn to accept myself. It's real hard but I think I'm getting there. In the long run, that's got to be worth it."

2

High Anxiety

Panic Attacks and Other Frightening Fears

*F*irst scenario: You're alone in the mountains hiking on a beautiful but remote trail. You bend down to tighten your bootlace. You look up again. Your eyes scan a forest of aspen trees. Their leaves shimmer and shake in the gentle wind. You breathe in the clear, sunny, fragrant mountain day and think to yourself, "This is heaven on earth." Suddenly you sense you are not alone. You look again to the trees and see a big, black bear staring at you. You freeze. It's hard to breathe—you feel like you're going to choke. Your heart starts beating so fast you feel it will pop out of your chest. You feel dizzy and light-headed. You start to sweat. All of a sudden the forest seems strange and unreal. Then the bear disappears into the trees. You catch your breath, turn around, and make your way back to the campsite where your family is still sleeping. You walk quickly. Your heart is still pounding, but when you see the familiar blue tents you relax and feel safe.

Second scenario: You're on your way to modern European history class—not your best subject. You feel a sense of dread, like you're a criminal in Napoleon's France on your way to the guillotine. In five minutes the teacher will hand you a unit test. You stayed up until 2 A.M. studying for this test and you're exhausted. You take your seat. The teacher plops the test down on your desk. You stare at the paper. You freeze. It's hard to breathe—you feel like you're going to choke. Your heart starts beating so fast you feel it will pop out of your chest. You feel dizzy and light-headed. You start to sweat. The classroom seems strange and unreal. The essay questions look like a blur of black letters on white paper. You ask the teacher if you can go to the bathroom to collect yourself but she says "no." You can't calm down, so you hand in a blank test. When the bell rings and you leave the classroom, you feel like you can breathe again. Your heart stops pounding. But you feel embarrassed and mortified to face the teacher the next day in class.

These scenarios are examples of anxiety reactions. The first scenario—in the mountains—shows a normal anxiety reaction (rapid heartbeat, shallow breathing, feeling dizzy, and so on) to a possible threat to your life. A normal anxiety reaction ends with a feeling of relief.

The second scenario—the history test—shows normal anxiety gone haywire. Your body and mind are responding to the history test as if it were a threat to your life. This is called a panic attack. Instead of feeling relieved and safe, a panic attack often leaves you feeling confused, afraid, and out of control.

Panic attacks are not uncommon. Most people have had the experience at one time or another. According to Dr. Denise F. Beckfield, author of *Master Your Panic and Take Back Your Life!*, you're more likely to suffer from panic attacks if you may be sensitive to separation from the people you love—like if you hate overnights away from your family, or if you never wanted your mom to leave you at school when you were little.

Stress and anxiety can trigger panic attacks. After September 11, 2001, the whole world's anxiety level rose a notch or two. Millions of Americans worried about getting on an airplane or about anthrax contaminating their mail. In the weeks following the World Trade Center and Pentagon attacks, lots of people had panic attacks, especially if they had to fly.

Panic attacks might also be genetic—if one of your parents has panic attacks, you might be prone to having them too.

When an anxiety reaction doesn't subside immediately, like in the first scenario, you can feel *over-*

whelmed even if you don't get a full-blown panic attack. Persistent anxiety—often called *generalized anxiety*—can make you feel nervous and jittery and worried all day and night. You may even become forgetful as a result of anxiety. You may get headaches or stomachaches. Sometimes anxiety makes a person develop obsessive-compulsive behaviors like constantly checking to make sure doors and windows are locked or washing her hands repeatedly during the day.

Panic attacks, generalized anxiety, and obsessive-compulsive behaviors can be really scary—you might feel like you're going to die or pass out. You might feel nauseous, like you're about to get sick. You might feel like you're going crazy. But try not to be afraid. Your anxiety reactions are just symptoms, and after all, symptoms aren't all bad. They tell you things. They let you know that you're upset about something, real or imagined. They remind you that you need to use calming-down skills to cope with your anxious feelings. They remind you to soothe yourself in stressful situations. And when you learn how to cope with anxiety and to soothe yourself successfully, your symptoms won't be so much of a problem anymore.

You can do lots of things to manage anxiety and panic attacks. You *can* take charge. You *can* calm down. You just need to learn how. And then you'll see just how strong and competent you really are. You won't believe how *good* you'll feel about yourself!

Here are the stories of how three girls calm down and cope. See if some of the things they do work for you too.

Rebecca

"I thought I was having a heart attack."

Rebecca is 15. She lives in a close, middle-class neighborhood. Rebecca's big family (three brothers and two sisters, all younger) is Orthodox Jewish and she goes to a Jewish day school. Sometimes Rebecca wishes she went to the public high school, but she doesn't bug her parents about this because it's important to them that she gets a Jewish education. After she graduates, Rebecca wants to go to a large state university where she'll meet all kinds of people.

Rebecca barely gets panic attacks anymore. But this was not always the case. When she was in seventh grade, she thought she'd drop dead before she was 13. Her panic attacks were *that* strong and terrifying.

I felt like no one's heart could take it—beating 200 times a minute, like a little bird. I truly thought I was going to die before my bat mitzvah, which was in June, and this all started in September.

Rebecca's panic attacks started around the time that her family moved from Chicago to the suburbs.

She had to go to a new school where she didn't know one person.

I missed my old friends—people I'd known since preschool. It was quite a shock. I was self-conscious because I'm really short, and I never felt like I looked cool enough. In middle school, girls can be so mean—they teased me about my hair. They all knew how to blow-dry their hair in cool styles. The only thing I knew to do with my hair was to put it in a ponytail and they called me "frizzball."

Rebecca got her first panic attack when she was about to get out of the car on the second week at her new school.

I woke up with a stomachache and didn't want to go to school but my mom said I had to go because I didn't have a fever. I felt sick in the car. When we got to school I couldn't breathe right. It felt like I was gasping for breath and I was dizzy and my heart was pounding so fast. I thought I was having an asthma attack even though I never had asthma. I just sat in the car crying and telling my mom I couldn't go. My mom didn't know what to do. She took me to the doctor and I calmed down in the waiting room. The nurse took my pulse and listened to my heart and said nothing was wrong physically. She said I had a panic attack. In a way I was relieved, but in a way I was embarrassed too. I had to go to school the next

*day and it was like torture because I had another
panic attack just before lunch. I went to the nurse's
office and lay down for a while—I told her I had a
stomachache. After about a half an hour I felt like I
could go back to class, but it was really horrible.*

Rebecca had several more panic attacks before she
finally got some help. Each one felt scarier and scarier.
But after she had several talks with her school social
worker, she got some good ideas about how to handle her panic attacks. She developed some panic-
attack strategies that work.

Belly Breathe

When you're having a panic attack, you tend to
breathe too fast. Deep breathing helps slow down
your breath, which calms your mind. But you have to
breathe from your diaphragm, not your chest. Some
people call this kind of breathing "belly breathing."

To belly breathe, put one hand on your belly.
Breathe in slowly through your nose, mouth closed.
Hold your breath for a second or two, then breathe out
slowly, again through your nose. Feel your belly rise
when you inhale and fall when you exhale. That's it!

*When I feel a panic attack coming on, I start
my belly breathing. It calms me down and distracts
me and sometimes I never get the panic attack. It
helps to count to myself when I'm doing my belly
breathing. With each breath I count:*

- *1 and 1 and*
- *2 and 1 and*
- *2 and 3 and 1 and*
- *2 and 3 and 4 and 1 and*
- *2 and 3 and 4 and 5 and 1*

You always go back to one. Counting and breathing help me concentrate on something else besides my panicky feelings. I feel more focused and then the panic doesn't get out of control.

Blow into a Paper Bag

Rebecca keeps a brown paper lunch bag in her backpack. If she feels panicky and light-headed at school, she goes into the bathroom and breathes with her paper bag around her mouth and nose. This gets less oxygen and more carbon dioxide to her brain, which helps ease the light-headedness. (Your brain could be getting too much oxygen during a panic attack because of rapid, shallow breathing and this can make you feel light-headed.)

Spin Around in Circles

When she first started working on her panic attacks, Rebecca's social worker asked her to stand up and spin around until she got dizzy. Then Rebecca sat down for a few minutes and discussed her feelings.

First I was really dizzy and then I wasn't dizzy anymore. That gave me a feeling that I had during a panic attack but it wasn't a panic attack. I learned that I could be dizzy and manage it. So when I get a

*real panic attack and feel dizzy, I know the dizziness
will go away, just like it does when I make myself
dizzy. Dizziness used to scare me because I felt so
weird and out of control. Now dizziness isn't such a
big deal. It actually doesn't scare me at all anymore.
I've learned how to tolerate it and that takes the fear
out.*

Carry a Cell Phone

When Rebecca gets a panic attack, or even if she's
afraid she might get a panic attack, it really helps to
connect with her family or a friend. So she carries a
cell phone when she has to go somewhere alone.

*If I can talk to someone, even on the phone, I feel
like I'm being pulled back into the real world, not my
"out there" world where I feel totally anxious and out
of control. I carry around my mom's cell phone. It
makes me feel secure, even though I don't even use it
that much. But I know that I can.*

Use Self-Talk

Rebecca talks to herself constantly when she gets a
panic attack. This helps her remember that the panic
attack will run its course—even though it feels
uncomfortable, it will pass through her. She reminds
herself that she *can* "ride out" the panic attack, and
that the end will come soon.

*I give myself what I call "calm-down talks." I
remind myself that it's just a stupid panic attack and*

it's nothing to worry about. I won't die. It will pass like it always does. Knowing I will survive is half the battle.

When I feel like a panic attack is coming, I immediately say to myself, "Breathe." That's a signal I give myself to start using my panic-attack strategies. Lots of times this will be enough to stop a full-blown panic attack.

The worst thing is to avoid things. That makes it worse. I didn't want to go back to school after my first panic attack and my mom let me stay home the rest of that day. But then I didn't want to go the next day either. I thought if I just didn't go to school I'd never get another panic attack. But she said it's like falling off a horse—you have to get back on or you'll be afraid of riding forever. In retrospect, I think she was right, even though I fought her about it at the time. If I had started staying home to avoid panic attacks, I might have had to have been home-schooled or something.

Self-talk also helps Rebecca figure out why she's having a panic attack because panic attacks are *always* related to feelings. She learned that her first panic attack was a result of feeling scared and out of control in a new situation—her new school.

I was scared of failing, of never making friends, of making a fool of myself. Now when I'm in new situations and I start to feel panicky, I ask myself

"What are you afraid of?" If I can figure out the feelings, it helps me understand the panic attack. It's like, "Oh, of course you feel panicky because you're trying something new for the first time." I used to feel sort of possessed, like my panic attacks were attacking me. I wish I wasn't susceptible to them but I am. But if I understand why I'm having them, it helps me feel more normal, like less of a freak. And it helps me feel more in control of them.

Can you think of reasons why you might have panic attacks? Hint: they usually have something to do with feeling out of control.

Mary

"I was panicked to get on a plane."

Mary is 14. She's a freshman at a big public high school. Mary has long hair down to her waist—she's never gotten a real haircut. She thinks it's the only thing that makes her special.

Ever since she can remember, Mary has hated to be away from her family. Once she tried to go to overnight camp when she was 12, but she was so miserable and homesick that she pretended she had migraines so she could come home after three days. Mary describes herself as a "fairly anxious person," but right after September 11, 2001, her anxiety began to feel like it rushed around inside her incessantly, like some huge and terrible wild beast.

For example, Mary has never exactly loved flying. Sometimes she'd get butterflies in her stomach before boarding a plane, but she did it anyway because she looked forward to going on vacations. But after the terrorist attacks, she never thought she'd get on a plane again—ever—for as long as she lived.

My dad flies all the time for work and he insisted that flying is still safe. He even got on a plane and flew to L.A. the week after the terrorist attacks. I was beginning to believe him, but then I saw on T.V. that a man almost got onto a plane with a briefcase full of knives and a stun gun. Then the newspaper said that flight attendants were scared to fly. Then there was another plane crash in New York a couple of months later. And then there's anthrax. Once I saw our mailman wearing latex gloves. I was afraid to open our mail. I was afraid I'd get anthrax on an airplane. I was afraid of terrorists crashing more planes. I was completely freaking out. I was a mess.

Mary's friends didn't seem to be too affected by the 9/11 attacks. Their attitudes were much more objective and less emotional than Mary's.

My good friends Leslee and Annie don't really understand why I'm so upset. They're both able to feel safe somehow. They feel bad that it happened and that people died, but their attitude is "we don't know anyone personally." It's not like they don't care—they just don't worry about it like I do. They don't think it will happen to them.

Mary's parents are typical of her relatively affluent community. Her dad works all the time and is away on business trips at least three days a week; her mom works in the public library part-time, but mostly stays home and takes care of Mary and her three younger sisters.

My mom is a little worried about my dad, I think. She doesn't say so, but she seems more anxious when he's gone and more relieved when he calls from out of town. But my mom isn't afraid of flying. I'm the only one in my family who is terrified.

Mary's fear of flying didn't interfere with her life too much—until Christmas vacation, 2001. Her family had plane tickets to fly to North Carolina from Chicago to visit her grandma. Needless to say, Mary did not want to travel by plane.

I begged my parents not to fly. I said we could drive. They wouldn't even talk about it with me. We were flying. I seriously didn't think this was fair of them to do to me, but I had no choice. I had to get on a plane or stay home with a babysitter and not see my grandma.

Here's how Mary calmed down and got on the plane.

Find a Reason

It was necessary for Mary to *decide* that it was *important to her* to go to North Carolina—that her desire to go see her grandma was stronger than her desire to stay home. This was crucial, because it gave her a deep-felt *reason* to get on the plane. We all need our own, personal reasons to change our behaviors. If we do something just because someone else wants us to, it's usually meaningless and doesn't work.

Seek Out Support

Once Mary acknowledged that it was important to her to see her grandma, she felt she needed massive doses of support from her parents. She needed them to tell her that everything would be OK.

At first my mom said that she could understand my fears because no one is really safe from terrorists, like it was the state of our world. This just made me cry. I needed her to tell me that we would land safely and that the airports are safe. I felt like a little baby, but I felt if she believed we would be OK, then I could believe it too.

When Mary told her mom that she was just making things worse with her talk about world terrorism, her mom was able to come through for her. Her mom reassured Mary that she truly believed everything would be OK and that she'd never put her children in danger. She said if she and Mary's dad didn't believe everything would be fine, they wouldn't go, pure and simple.

After that conversation, I kind of saw my parents as pillars of strength that I could lean on when I got scared about the flight. That helped a lot. It helped me put my fears away and not think about them so much, which was exactly what I needed.

Act Normal

Mary thought about the importance of getting on with her normal activities. She saw the value of trying not to let the terrorists *terrorize her* into doing things she normally wouldn't do, like avoiding planes. Normally, she would pack her backpack with a CD headset, magazines, crossword puzzles, and playing cards to distract herself from her anxiety about flying. She told herself that this trip was a normal thing for her family to do and prepared for it like she would under normal circumstances—like before September 11.

At first I wanted my mom to call my uncle, who's a doctor, and get me tranquilizers for the plane. I just wanted to sleep the whole way. But then I talked myself out of it. I said to myself, "That would be stupid and what if you got sick or something." Everyone says to get back to your normal routine, and my backpack has always been my security blanket on planes. So I packed it the way I normally would, with all my stuff. I also sat next to my dad, which I always do.

Analyze the Statistical Probability

Mary's good at math. She used this strength to help herself feel less afraid. She figured out that it was statistically extremely unlikely that a terrorist would be on *her* plane, that she would get anthrax in an airplane, and so on.

I know that it's more likely to get in a car crash than in an airplane crash and I expanded on that concept. I thought about the fact that the terrorist attacks happened to only a few flights out of thousands that took off that morning. I thought that there are 50 states in the U.S., and only 3 were affected. I thought about how only a few people got anthrax out of the hundreds of millions of people in our country, and that no one's come down with it in a long time. And no one's ever gotten anthrax on an airplane, so I probably won't be the first. These ideas helped me calm down and put things in perspective.

Pray

One more thing: Mary made up two prayers—one for when she boarded the plane and another prayer of thanks for when she landed safely.

I'm not a super religious person, but these were my prayers:

- *Dear God, please let this plane be safe and let there be only good people on it.*
- *Dear God, thank you for the safety of this trip.*

These little prayers helped me feel a little more comforted, like maybe God would be watching. It also helped to think that my grandma was waiting for us in North Carolina. That was definitely a reassuring thought.

I think that all of these things helped me cope with my anxiety. But the best thing of all was when we did *land safely and had a great vacation. The plane ride home wasn't quite as scary because I had been through it all before. Since nothing bad happened on the way there, I could relax a little and believe that nothing would happen on the way home, which was the truth. Everything was fine.*

Laura

"I always worried about things, every day."

Laura is 16. She's pretty athletic; she likes to play field hockey and loves snowboarding. Her family visits her grandparents every Christmas in Colorado, so she gets to snowboard a lot over her winter break.

Laura used to suffer from generalized anxiety. She was worried about absolutely *everything*. She worried if someone didn't say "hi" to her in the hall. ("I thought they hated me.") She worried about her 18-

year-old brother's acne. ("He's washing his face with the wrong stuff—he's going to get permanent scars.") She worried about her father dying of a heart attack. ("He eats red meat all the time, and I know that's bad for his heart.")

I was anxious all the time. It was like my mind was churning out these horrible thoughts and I had no way to stop them. I'd worry for days about what I said to a boy I liked, like it was the stupidest thing ever said. I constantly worried about my grades and whether they were good enough to get into college. I'd feel really tense all day. I developed a habit of clenching my teeth and grinding them at night. My dentist had to make me a mouth guard so I wouldn't ruin my teeth. Now it sounds silly and I realize I was just driving myself crazy with all the worrying. But at the time it was very hard to deal with my anxious feelings.

Laura also had obsessive-compulsive thoughts and behaviors. She did lots of little rituals to put her mind at ease.

I had to check that the doors were locked three times before I went to bed. It didn't matter if my parents were home and said that they'd already locked the doors. I had to see for myself. I also hated the number one for some reason. I think it's because I thought that one is so lonely. I always put my stuffed animals in groups so that none of them was alone. And I had to make sure I said "Good night, sleep tight" to my parents and my brother. I couldn't get to sleep at night if I didn't say that.

Laura has a friend who has serious problems with anxiety and obsessive-compulsive behavior. She has to take medication. Laura didn't want to take medication if she didn't have to. She developed some ingenious ways to stave off her anxiety. Here are her tips. They work well for her. Try them. Maybe they'll work for you too.

Ingenious Tip #1: The Shoe-Box Solution

One day, while Laura was thumbing through one of her mom's old textbooks, she read that, according to Eastern philosophy, "energy follows thought."

That made me think about myself. I realized that my worrying wasn't helping anything, and that it was just putting negative energy in my life. Now I write down my worries on scraps of paper. Even in the middle of the night! I keep a pencil and paper by my bed and when I worry, I write down my feelings. It kind of helps me put my worries away so I can get to sleep. I throw all the scraps of paper into a shoe box I keep in my closet. And once a month I read them and see that none of them has materialized. Then I throw them in the trash. This helps get rid of worries—literally!

Ingenious Tip #2: Coping Quotations

Laura also found a quotation by Mark Twain that she repeats to herself every day. She made three copies and taped one on the inside of her assignment notebook, put one on her bedroom mirror, and carries one in her wallet. It says, "I have spent most of my life worrying about things that have never happened."

"Now I love looking for inspiring quotations. I started a quotation journal. It's really cool." Here's a sample from Laura's quotation journal:

> "Whether you believe you can do a thing or not, you are right."—Henry Ford
> "I am not afraid of storms for I am learning how to sail my ship."—Louisa May Alcott
> "The way I see it, if you want the rainbow, you gotta put up with the rain."—Dolly Parton
> "Your holiest moments, most sacred moments, are often the ones that are most painful."—Oprah Winfrey
> "Don't be afraid your life will end. Be afraid that it will never begin."—Grace Hansen

Ingenious Tip #3: Aromatherapy

Laura bought some lavender oil at a candle shop and put a few drops on a cotton ball. She carries this in her backpack.

I read about this in a magazine. Lavender is supposed to be relaxing. So when I get tense and anxious at school, I smell my cotton ball. No one sees because I hide it in my hand. I pretend I'm scratching my nose or something. It really does help me calm down—maybe it's all psychological, but it really does help me.

Ingenious Tip #4: A Rainbow of Protection

When Laura feels anxious, she imagines a giant rainbow is above her, protecting her and giving her hope.

I call it my rainbow of protection. The image is comforting to me and reminds me that beautiful things are in my life and I don't have to get stuck in my anxiety. I like to think that my anxious thoughts are floating above the clouds and getting lost in my rainbow. Now all I have to do is think about my rainbow and I feel calmer.

Laura has also made some headway in dealing with obsessive-compulsive behaviors. This hasn't been easy because some of the rituals have been going on for years. She thinks these ideas have helped:

Focus on the Positive

Some of Laura's obsessive-compulsive behaviors are positive, like always putting on a seat belt when she gets in a car, always looking both ways before she crosses a street, always checking her homework on spell-check, always brushing and flossing her teeth before bed, always making her lunch before she goes to bed at night so she won't have to rush in the morning—things like that. So she feels good about being a little "compulsive."

Backbend the Mind

Laura has a flexible body. She can stand and do a backbend to the floor. When she feels the urge to do obsessive-compulsive behaviors that annoy her, she thinks about making her mind as flexible as her spine.

Checking the doors is a stupid habit because sometimes I'm in bed and I realize that I forgot to check the doors so I get up and do it even though what I really want to do is relax in my cozy bed. And the "good night, sleep tight" is so babyish.

Then I was sick a few months ago and I seriously couldn't get out of bed to check the doors. I had the flu and I slept from 4 in the afternoon until 11 the next morning. I asked my mom if I checked the doors at night, and she said no. It occurred to me that nothing bad happened and that I could stop my compulsion to check. It would be OK. Now when I get the urge, I remember that night when I was sick. It helps me resist. I still check the doors before I go upstairs to bed most of the time, but I never get out of bed to do it three times anymore.

It feels good to have a more flexible mind. It feels like a big relief. Even though when I get stressed out I sometimes revert back to my old behaviors, I think I'm making progress.

Think About the "Why"

Laura also realized that she is prone to anxiety because of a life event that happened when she was seven. Her mom had breast cancer. It was caught in an early stage and she's in excellent health now, but at the time Laura was very, very scared.

> *Mom had a great attitude and she kept on saying everything would be fine. But she had to have radiation and I remember she was tired all the time and couldn't play with me or take me to school. I think that's when my checking-the-doors behavior started. And that's when I started feeling scared of bad things happening.*
>
> *It helps to think that there was a reason for all my anxiety. Now if I find myself worrying about every little thing, I can say to myself, "Calm down! You're not seven anymore! Mom's well. Get over it! Everything's OK!" Not that it's easy, but it does help to tell myself to calm down.*

Summing It Up

Panic attacks, generalized anxiety, and obsessive-compulsive behaviors are all anxiety reactions that can make you feel terrible. But they don't have to be permanent obstacles in your life. No matter how "haywire" your anxiety reactions are, you can learn to cope with them—and in many cases, erase them from your life altogether. Try some of the new behaviors in this chapter. Maybe some of them will work for you too.

Initially, anxiety reactions usually don't come "out of the blue"—each girl had a real-life reason for feeling anxious in the first place. Mary's fear of flying was a reaction to the terrorist attacks on September 11, 2001. Rebecca and Laura had deeper, more personal reasons for their anxiety reactions—Rebecca's were related to leaving all her old friends and starting a new school in seventh grade; Laura's had to do with her mom's battle with breast cancer.

Are you introspective? Do you think about *why* you do certain things? Then try to figure out the real-life reason behind your anxiety. Talk to yourself about it. Like Rebecca, Mary, and Laura, your insight might help you.

Or maybe you're the type who just likes to *do* things instead of trying to figure out *why*. Try some of Rebecca's panic-attack strategies, or Laura's ingenious tips to calm down.

Are you spiritual? Make up a little prayer to calm yourself, like Mary did.

Are you good at imagining and visualizing? Try Laura's rainbow of protection technique.

Do you like to surf the web? Try this website for ideas on how to deal with panic and anxiety: panic disorder.about.com/cs/copingwith911/index.htm.

Have panic attacks and like to read? Lots of good self-help books are out there. Look around in your library or bookstore—you might find several that will be helpful. Rebecca likes *Master Your Panic and Take Back Your Life!* by Denise Beckfield. (See Resources for Your Journey at the back of the book.)

Sometimes anxiety can be so *totally* overwhelming that you can barely function in your life. If this happens to you—no matter how hard you try to cope with your feelings—and lasts for more than a week, you should ask your parents if you can see a counselor or therapist.

Remember, Rebecca found ways to deal with her panic attacks, Mary found ways to get on a plane, and Laura found ways to deal with her high anxiety feelings and behaviors. And *you* can learn to conquer your fears and lead a normal life too.

As Laura says, "I still get anxious a lot. I still get a little obsessive-compulsive. But I'm learning to live with it. My mom says life's not worry-free. Everyone gets anxious sometimes. It's being able to do things anyway that matters. That makes sense to me and it helps."

The Sun Through the Clouds

When You Feel Down

*E*ver wonder why you didn't feel depressed when you were younger? It's because your brain actually changes when you become an adolescent. You have the capacity to think abstractly, whereas little kids think concretely. A four-year-old child will see a man dancing in the street and think he's funny, maybe a clown; you will understand that he could be either drunk or mentally ill. For the first time, you can reflect on yourself and ask yourself things like "what is the purpose of my life?" You can question the deeper meaning of a poem; you can understand that life is unfair.

"I feel sad." "I'm so unhappy." "My life sucks." Who doesn't feel sad or down from time to time? Lots of things can make you feel this way. When you feel temporarily down, you are most likely experiencing *situational depression*. Situational depression means what it says: feeling depressed because of a situation—something *happened or is happening* to make you sad. Sometimes the situation is obvious, like you're not getting along with your friends, the boy you like doesn't like you, your parents fight a lot, or someone you love is sick.

And sometimes the situation isn't so obvious—you think, "I have nothing to be depressed about but I feel down." You might be more upset than you think about some small but meaningful event, like being klutzy on the volleyball court or not being invited to a party. From time to time you have to search your thoughts, feelings, and experiences for the clues to your depression.

Usually, you experience whatever happened as a *loss* of some sort—for example, the loss of a relationship, the loss of an award you wanted really badly, the loss of control, or the fear that someone may die or get divorced. Situational depression usually gets better in a few weeks, unless the situation persists.

If you feel depressed for more than two weeks, or feel depressed "out of the blue," you may *not* have situational depression. Instead of being related to situations, depression can be biological (caused by brain chemistry imbalances). This type of depression can be hereditary. Does your mom or dad take antidepressants? Has a close relative been hospitalized for depression or bipolar disorder (manic-depression)? If the answer is "yes," biological depression may run in your family.

Depression can also be low grade and chronic. For example, if someone you love has cancer, you will probably feel depressed for a while. You may be able to function well in school and go out with friends, but you may feel an underlying dull ache of sadness.

If you've felt sad for months, or if you feel sad for *no reason*, cut or scratch yourself, pick at your face, or *think a lot about suicide*, you may have a biological or chronic depression. *Talk to your parents about seeing a therapist.* Hope and help are definitely out there for you, but first you have to tell someone how *bad* you feel. You can also check out the website nostigma .com. It's the website of the National Mental Health Awareness Campaign and it will tell you more about biological and chronic depression.

Low self-esteem can increase your likelihood of feeling down. In fact, in his bestseller, *Feeling Good*, Dr. David Burns recommends that you set aside time every day to work on improving your self-esteem. As you will see in the following stories, there are lots of interesting and creative ways to do this.

Even though situational depression is a normal part of life and goes away with time, it's not a trivial condition. Here are some common feelings and behaviors you may have:

- You may feel like you hate your life.
- You may feel like a loser or like nothing goes your way.

- You may feel crushed, emotionally *and* physically; you may get stomachaches; or you may feel shaky and distressed, like you just got run over by a truck.
- Your energy may feel zapped. You may feel unmotivated to do your homework or go out with friends.
- Your appetite may not feel normal. You may not feel hungry at all, or you may eat nonstop.
- Your sleep habits may be changed. You may feel like sleeping all day, or you may not be able to get to sleep even though it's way past your bedtime.
- You may lose important things, like your watch or the key to your house.
- You may be easily annoyed and overly analytical. For example, you may question the motives of others. You may interpret benign comments as personal attacks.
- You may feel like you're just going through the motions of your day, like you're just a shell of your normal self.
- You may cry way too easily.
- You may know in your mind that you have good things in your life, but you don't *feel* that way.

Situational depression is not life threatening but it can be life disrupting, like a thunderstorm. The dark clouds will pass and the sun will come out again—it always does. But in the meantime, you can learn to wait out the rain. You can discover lots of ways to tolerate and soothe your bad feelings. In fact, the more ways you have to comfort yourself, the more protected you will be from the storm of situational depression.

So build a strong shelter! Make it as big as possible and stock it with shelves of soothing stuff!

Here are the stories of how three girls cope with feeling down.

Kelly

"I couldn't stop crying because of my boyfriend."

Kelly is 15 and from a huge Irish Catholic family— nine brothers and sisters! Her mom stays home to take care of her twin baby sisters and volunteers at her parish. Her dad works long hours—Kelly wishes she saw more of him. In all, six kids are still living at home, ages 1 to 17.

Kelly got depressed when her boyfriend of two-and-a-half months broke up with her at a party and immediately hooked up with another girl. She found them kissing in the bathroom and was understandably upset and humiliated.

I felt like someone kicked me in the stomach. When I got home from the party, I just went in my room and cried and cried. I couldn't eat all weekend. Luckily, my parents understood. They didn't make me

eat breakfast with the family the next morning—my
mom brought me some toast and juice to my room
instead. I just wanted to sleep all day. That's what I
did, all weekend.

I couldn't believe my boyfriend would do this,
ever. I thought I knew him and I thought he was
nice. I thought I could trust him. But I guess I was
wrong. Obviously.

By the next weekend, Kelly felt a little better. She
could eat and sleep and was back to her normal self,
practically. She had talked with her friends and everybody agreed her ex-boyfriend was a jerk and that he
was just using the girl he hooked up with (he never
even called her after that). Talking to her friends definitely gave Kelly some much-needed support. But she
also did some other things that kept her self-esteem
from plummeting.

Here's what helped Kelly get through the breakup.

No More Lady Godiva

Kelly decided that her drastic situation required drastic measures. Three weeks after the breakup, she cut
her waist-length hair to just below her shoulders.
Kelly had been thinking about doing this for months,
but her boyfriend loved her long hair. So what better
time could there be?

It felt like a weight was lifted off of me, literally. I
went with a friend, and we both loved it. And my
boyfriend never wanted me to cut my hair, so I

showed him! It felt great to see him do a double take in the halls last week! I wish I could frame the expression on his face—it was hilarious.

A Room Rearrangement

Kelly also changed her bedroom around. She removed pictures of her boyfriend from the wall above her bed and threw them in a box that ended up in the attic. She painted her room "spring green" all by herself (she got that idea from reading the late dancer Isadora Duncan's autobiography, *My Life*). She moved her bed to the opposite wall and moved her desk where her bed used to be. She put up a big bulletin board and tacked up rock posters that she bought off the Internet.

I feel like I need a fresh start. If I can't have him, at least I can do something new for myself. That's what my room represents to me. A new life. I feel much better now. I still get a knot in my stomach when I see him around, but at least I can laugh again. And I love my hair!

"The More Corn and Cheese, the Better"

Kelly loves to listen to corny songs and watch cheesy movies and television shows when she feels down and upset. They make her laugh, which makes her relax and feel better.

My sister and I have this joke about a song that's so stupid. I forgot the name but the words are "Don't worry, be happy!" It's like a reggae song. It's so upbeat and corny, it's impossible not to laugh.

I also like movies like Crossroads *with Britney Spears or* Legally Blonde *with Reese Witherspoon. They're so cheesy and dumb, but when you're upset, it's exactly what you need. Or sometimes I watch cartoons, like "The Simpsons." They make me laugh.*

A Heating Pad

Sometimes Kelly gets a stomachache when she feels tense and upset and depressed. Her soothing remedy? Kelly snuggles up in bed with a good book and a heating pad on her tummy. The heat loosens up the tension in her stomach and helps her calm down and feel better.

Sometimes when I'm alone, I feel really sad and tense—like something's squeezing my stomach— when I think about my old boyfriend. I know it's because I'm still upset. So if I'm home, I'll just put on my pajamas, plug in my heating pad, and get into bed. I have an electrical outlet in the wall in back of my bed, so I prop up pillows against my headboard and sit with the heating pad on my stomach. I sit like this, reading, for about 15 or 20 minutes, sometimes more. It relaxes me—this is a very good thing for me to do.

The Lake Solution

Kelly is lucky. She lives near a big lake. One of her most favorite ways to feel better is to go to the lake and look at the waves. They remind her that things change because waves, like feelings, don't stay the same. They both come and go, ebb and flow. This idea helps Kelly gain perspective on her feelings—it helps her know that her sad feelings will change, and this helps her tolerate them for the time being.

I love to just sit there by myself. I love how the lake changes color when a cloud covers the sun. I love how the waves come to the shore and make a whooshing *sound. I imagine that my anger and my sadness are being washed away into the lake. Washed away from my brain. I feel peaceful when I'm at the lake.*

Tameeka

"I know I should be happy but I'm so sad."

Tameeka is 16. She has one brother, two dogs, and two parents. Her dad is a nurse and her mom is a teacher. Tameeka just got her driver's license and the only problem is that her family now has four drivers and one car. Her parents don't feel they need another car since they both take the train to work, but Tameeka and her brother are trying to save up for one themselves.

Tameeka feels depressed from time to time, but until recently she had no idea why. On the outside, her life's going great: Her grades are good. She gets along fine with her family. She has lots of friends at school. But a sad feeling inside kept gnawing at her.

I really had no idea what was wrong. I felt like my friends expected this outgoing, kind of crazy person and I just couldn't be like that anymore. I wasn't myself. I felt like I wasn't fun to be around, and that made me feel even worse.

Here's how Tameeka figured out why she felt down.

Three Questions

Tameeka became very curious about her sad feelings. She kept on asking herself, "why now?" Then she thought of these three questions to ask herself.

1. Are there any changes at home?
2. Are there any changes with friends?
3. Are there certain times I feel more or less depressed?

At first I thought that nothing had changed. But then I realized two things. One is that my best friend got a boyfriend and I don't see very much of her anymore because she spends all her time with him. I guess I feel a little replaced by him and a little jealous that she has a boyfriend and I don't. The other thing is that my mom gets depressed before her period, and I think I get the most depressed just before my period too.

If I know there's a reason that I feel depressed, I feel a lot better. I talked with my mom and she told me some things she does when she feels depressed before her period, like cutting back on caffeine and trying to relax and take it easy. My mom said she gets more depressed in the winter when there's not so much sunlight, and I think that's true for me too because I feel better on a sunny day. Anyway, when I feel depressed before my period, I always tell myself, "you feel down because you're PMSing. You'll feel better in a few days." And I usually do.

And I told my best friend that I miss going out with her like we used to, like to the mall or to a movie. I tried to put it in a positive way, not that I was jealous but that I missed her. She said that her boyfriend goes out with his guy friends and she wants to go out with her girlfriends more now too. So it was good to talk to her about how I felt.

Creative E-Mailing

Tameeka hates journaling because it takes too much time and effort to handwrite her ideas on the blank page of a book. But she loves E-mailing her friends—writing E-mails relaxes her.

Then Tameeka had a brainstorm. Why not write E-mails to herself? So she set up a private E-mail account. Now when she feels sad or confused or depressed, she E-mails letters (some of them very long) to herself. This process helps her sort out her feelings and gain a clearer perspective of what's bothering her.

I'm always on the computer so sometimes I take a study break and E-mail myself a letter. No one else can read it because they don't know my password. The account is free too, so I don't have to ask for money from my parents or anything. My E-mail account is with hotmail.com but I think there are other places too, like yahoo.com.

I just type and type until my feelings are all on the screen, right in front of me. It helps me understand myself better. And I like the feeling of clicking the send button when I'm done, like I'm purging myself of all these sad feelings and they're flying out into my secret corner in cyberspace.

Tameeka also found creative ways to *nurture herself*—and they help heal her depressed feelings and helped her feel better about herself.

Something's Cooking

Tameeka likes to help her parents prepare meals. She has always found cooking and baking to be relaxing and creative outlets. Tameeka prides herself on her homemade vegetable soup.

One Saturday night I was all alone because, of course, my best friend was out with her boyfriend. I didn't know what to do. I felt depressed and bored. Then I got out my soup pot and started chopping vegetables. I made a big pot of delicious soup. And I had a big bowl, with a bagel. It felt very good to

*make my soup and to eat it—like I was feeding
myself in a good way. I guess I could have made
brownies or cookies, and I do that sometimes too, but
I just felt like soup that night.*

Tameeka discovered that cooking is a good creative outlet for her. Cooking something feels soothing and special—like a present to herself. And it's a big hit with her family. Now when she feels depressed, cooking is one of her solutions.

*I feel calm and content, looking around the
kitchen, deciding what to put in my soup, stirring it,
seasoning it. I feel very creative and in charge. It
even feels good to clean up afterward—I like getting
my hands soapy, making things clean. My feelings
are definitely brighter after I cook something.*

Here's Tameeka's soup recipe. Don't be afraid to improvise. Substitute vegetables and spices. Add leftover chicken, turkey, beef, or pasta. Add diced tofu. Be creative!

Tameeka's Vegetable Soup

1 quart canned chicken stock (or water)
1 potato, peeled and diced
2 carrots, peeled and sliced
2 celery stalks, sliced
1 onion, chopped

2 cloves garlic, chopped
1 can of chopped tomatoes, including the juice
1 teaspoon dried thyme
½ teaspoon salt
Dash of pepper

Put chicken stock in a big pot. Cook on high heat until it boils. Add the rest of the ingredients. Turn down heat to low, cover partially with a lid, and simmer for about an hour (stirring occasionally) until potato is soft. Enjoy!

Tameeka also wants to share her family's recipe for brownies:

Tameeka's Brownies

1 8-ounce box unsweetened chocolate (Tameeka
   uses Baker's brand)
3 sticks butter
3 cups sugar
6 eggs
3 teaspoons vanilla
1½ cups flour

Preheat oven to 350°F. Grease and flour two 8-inch square pans. Melt chocolate and butter in double boiler on stove. (This can also be done in a microwave.) Cool. Beat sugar and eggs together. Add to cooled chocolate mixture. Stir in vanilla. Add flour and mix lightly. Pour into 2 prepared pans and bake around 25–30 minutes, until toothpick inserted in center comes out clean. Cool, cut, and enjoy!

Plans with Other Friends: Just Do It!

Friendships are *nurturing to our souls*—having a friend means having someone to talk to, having someone to share activities with, and having someone to feel close to. Tameeka was used to doing everything with her best friend, but in fact there were plenty of other friends to hang out with. She just had to pick up the phone and call them!

It was definitely hard at first because I didn't want to be the one calling people all the time. I felt like they'd think I was needy and pathetic. But once I started calling other girls to see if they wanted to make plans for the weekend, I found out that things worked out. In a few weeks, people were calling me.

Before my best friend got her boyfriend, everyone assumed that we always did things together so no one really called me to invite me to do things. But now, since I called them, *that's changed. I still do things with my best friend, but now I have other people that I do things with too.*

Treats for the Senses

Just before she gets her period, when Tameeka often feels down, she likes to surround herself with beautiful things. Nothing big or expensive—just small mementos and little treats—to remind herself that no matter what, beauty is still in her life. She feels beautiful things nurture her senses—sight, touch, sound, taste, and smell—and this helps her feel calmer inside.

It could be a card I send to myself, a new pen in a cool color, a candle—anything, really. I love rose incense. I found some called "Amma's Rose" online. It costs $2.00 per package. It is absolutely the best incense. It makes my room smell like roses. I love listening to a classical CD called Handel's Water Music. It's very beautiful. I like to make myself some tea and bring it up to my room. I put a lot of honey in it and that's how I like it. Little things like that help me feel better, especially when I'm PMSing.

Being close to nature makes me feel better, too. Summer's my favorite time of year and I find little stones at the beach. Sometimes I find beach glass— glass the water makes smooth. I have a little collection now. I think I have about 12 pieces from the beach. I put them on a little glass shelf I have in my room. The colors are so pretty. I look at them and they make me think of the summer. That helps me feel better, even if it's just for a minute or two. I like collecting red and yellow and orange leaves in the fall too. I pin them to my bulletin board.

Sami

"I was very close to my grandma. When she died it was like I lost my best friend."

Sami is 16 and describes herself as a "mountain girl." She visited Montana a couple of years ago with her family and fell in love with the mountains. Sami loves hiking, camping, rafting, skiing—everything she loves is all about the mountains. Her dad is an outdoorsman, and Sami and her younger brother get to go on camping trips with him every year.

Sami became depressed after her Grandma Samantha died. They were born on the same day, and Sami was named in her honor.

I adored my grandma. I couldn't imagine life without her. When I had homework, she'd always be there to help me. She'd even type my papers if I asked her to. She baked me chocolate chip cookies without the chocolate chips because that's how I like them. I just loved her so much.

Sami's grandma died at the beginning of summer vacation, just after Sami's freshman year of high school. She was diagnosed with cancer, but the doctor said she would live at least three years. But two weeks later, Grandma Samantha was rushed to the hospital and died the next day.

That really tore me apart. She was old, but not that old. She was 70 when she died. I never expected her to die before I went to college. I was incredibly sad. I thought I'd never get over it.

Sami was extremely close to her grandma, and of course it was normal for her to feel depressed when she died. But Sami knew Grandma Samantha would want her to get on with her life. So Sami found some ways to mourn—and make it through—her grandmother's death.

Rent a Movie and Go with the (Feeling) Flow

All feelings are temporary—they ebb and flow. But when you're depressed, it can seem like they're permanent. At first, Sami tried to block her feelings—she was afraid that she'd have a total mental breakdown if she allowed herself to cry even one tear. But after talking to a friend who had also lost a grandparent, she realized that it was important to cry and let the feelings out. The sadness actually became *less* intense after Sami had a good cry—feelings are *most powerful* when we hold them inside.

I felt so bottled up, I couldn't cry. I was afraid to start because I thought I'd never stop crying for the rest of my life.

Then my friend gave me an idea. She said to rent a sad movie and I'd probably start crying and it would be good for me. So I did. I rented an old one— On Golden Pond. I started crying at the end, of course. You can't not cry at the end of that movie. I probably sounded insane but it didn't matter because no one was home. I just let it all out. I was really crying for my Grandma Samantha. It lasted for probably 10 minutes. It felt like a big relief when I stopped, like a weight was lifted from me. That's how it felt.

A Memory Table

Sami has lots of pictures of Grandma Samantha. She also has her grandma's pearls and a couple of bracelets and handkerchiefs. Sami decided to put all these things on a little bench, which she calls Grandma Samantha's Memory Table. It helps her think of her grandma and all the good times they shared. Sami feels that her grandma is with her in spirit, especially when she looks at the Memory Table.

I found a little table in our basement. I painted it pale lavender. Then I found some material at the store that was flowery and had little kittens on it. Grandma always loved cats. I got about a yard and folded it in half and put it over the table so it draped down a little. I put Grandma's pictures in white plastic frames and put them on the table. I put her jewelry in a white ceramic bowl on one side. I put her handkerchiefs on the other side.

The whole table makes me think of my grandma, and it makes me feel good. I had fun doing it, and I think she'd be proud of me.

A Tree for Grandma

For her 16th birthday, Sami asked her parents if she could plant a tree in Grandma Samantha's memory. Her parents had no problem with this idea. Sami went with her mom to the garden center, and they picked out a little crab apple tree. They found the perfect place in the backyard for it, and Sami's mom said that the flowers would be really gorgeous.

The tree is just another reminder of my grandma. Every time I look out the kitchen window, I see it and I think of her.

Summing It Up

Kelly, Tameeka, and Sami all felt down because of some *hard times.* Kelly had to cope with being rejected by a jerky boyfriend; Tameeka had to cope with feeling replaced by her best friend's boyfriend, and also with premenstrual depression; Sami had to cope with the death of her beloved grandma. All the situations were different, yet each situation represented a *loss* to the girl involved.

All three girls devised solutions to ease their sadness. For Kelly, that meant, in part, creating lots of *change* in her life—her hair, the color of her room, her furniture configuration, her wall decorations—she changed them all, and this helped her feel more in control of her life. Also, songs, cartoons, and movies that made her *laugh* and *relax* helped Kelly tolerate the temporary pain of the breakup.

Before Tameeka could deal with her depressed feelings, she had to figure out where they were coming from. Her three questions helped her pinpoint the reasons she was down. E-mailing letters to herself was another good way to explore and release her feelings.

Tameeka found that *nurturing herself* helped her cope with her depressed feelings. She cooked and baked and surrounded herself with beautiful things in her room like incense, flowers, candles, beautiful stones, music, and delicious tea. (If you too like incense, try Amma's Rose. It's listed in Resources for Your Journey.)

Tameeka also nurtured herself by cultivating new friendships to help fill up the empty time in her life— time she used to spend with her best friend. Kelly's heating pad is another good way to nurture yourself. (Just be sure not to fall asleep with it on!)

Some people nurture themselves by painting their toenails. Others nurture themselves by giving themselves a facial or deep conditioning their hair. Be creative! What's the best way *you can nurture yourself?*

It was important for Sami to let her feelings of loss *come out* before she could feel better about her grandma's death. Crying was the first step. Then she found creative outlets for her sadness, like creating the memory table and planting the crab apple tree.

Try some of these solutions for yourself. They'll help you discover new *solutions of your own.* Practice makes perfect—it's true. So don't give up. With perseverance and practice, you *will* find ways to soothe *your* down feelings too.

As Kelly says, "Sometimes I wonder why my boyfriend just dumped me for someone else. I get scared something's wrong with me. But I try not to dwell on that. I try not to get down on myself. My sister said, 'sometimes you just have to grin and bear it because what doesn't kill you makes you stronger.' That's how I'm looking at it—it will make me stronger. You think you'll never feel better, ever, but actually you do. It just takes a while."

Venus to Mars

Dealing with Guys

*D*oes thinking about guys drive you crazy? Are you curious about having a boyfriend, but clueless as to what it means to be in a relationship? If you have a boyfriend, are his desires and behavior perplexing? Well, join the club of girls who feel like you. Dealing with a guy can be more complicated than dealing with a whole different gender. It can feel like you're dealing with someone from a whole different galaxy!

When you were little, you could play with boys and it wasn't a big deal—as long as you could agree on what game or sport to play. But now *everything's different*. Your actual *brain chemistry* is different. For the

first time you can think in abstractions. You can wonder, "what would it be like to . . . " or "if I say this, people might think . . . " You worry about things you
never even used to think about. You have new sexual
sensations and fantasies that may feel dangerously
exciting. And you're most likely confused as hell about
how to read—and how to behave around—guys.

And for good reason. It's scary to like someone.
It's scary to want to have a relationship. For one
thing, he may not like you the way you like him. Or
you may think you're attracted to him but then
change your mind. It's hard to be rejected—but it's
also hard when you know you're the one who's
inflicting pain on someone else.

But there are also payoffs to having a boyfriend.
It feels really good to know that someone cares about
you and thinks you're cute. It can boost your self-
confidence to know that a boy you like thinks you're
funny and have a good personality. It can make you
feel good about your body to know that he thinks
you're "hot." As Alice says in *The Go Ask Alice Book of
Answers*, a romance can help us "feel safe, understood, special, sexy, desirable, and physically ecstatic.
We can also experience the pleasure of someone else
feeling this way with us." So relationships with guys
can be worth the risk.

But what do you say? How do you act? Do *you* call
him? Do you tell your friends to tell *him* to call you?
Should you go on a date, or do you think that's
"dorky"? What if you're too shy to talk to him?
Should you hook up with a boy that you like but

don't know very well? Should you have sex with a boy if you love each other—what do you do?

Here are the answers that three girls found to these questions—and more. Read their stories. Maybe you can get some ideas on how *you* can deal with guys too.

Sarah

"I turned bright red every time I saw him. It was so embarrassing."

Sarah is 14 and lives with her parents and two younger sisters in a suburb of Chicago. She has a few close friends who are from different "groups," but Sarah doesn't consider herself a "group" person.

My best friend is in the "theater" group—she wants to be an actress. Another close friend is a "jock." She's going to try for a college scholarship in field hockey. Another friend goes to parties every weekend—I guess she's in the "partying" group. So I'm called a "floater." I have friends in all kinds of groups.

Until recently, Sarah never had a real boyfriend—although she's had lots of crushes on guys.

So many girls share Sarah's dilemma: How do you get a boy to like you? She had a crush on a boy in her math class—but she was too embarrassed to talk to him.

It was horrible. I'd just look down at my books when he walked past my desk to get to his seat, which was right in back of me. I was terrified of him, but I thought he was so cute and I wanted to talk to him so bad! We didn't hang out with the same friends so I couldn't really find out if he liked me through friends. The only time I saw him was in my math class and sometimes in the halls and at lunch. I didn't know what to do.

Here's what Sarah figured out to do about her crush.

Morphing Nervousness into Excitement

Sarah felt stupid for being so nervous and ignoring her crush. But then a friend asked her a question: Does feeling *excited* feel any different from feeling nervous? The answer was surprising, even to Sarah—and helped her calm down.

When I thought about it that way, I realized that I get the same fluttery feelings when I'm excited as I do when I get nervous. I get butterflies in my stomach. And I can't stop thinking about the situation. So my friend said, "Just tell yourself you're excited and not a nervous wreck." So that's what I did. This helped me feel better. And I think it's true—sometimes I do confuse my feelings of excitement with feelings of fear and nervousness.

Make Eye Contact and Smile

Even though she was scared to death to do it, Sarah got up the nerve to look her crush in the eye—and *smile* at him. Her reasoning was how would he know she was interested in him if she didn't even look at him? Plus, the worst-case scenario? He'd ignore her just like she'd been ignoring him, so she really wouldn't lose anything. As you can see, this approach worked to her advantage.

Just smiling at him sounds too lame to be a solution, but it was an important step for me. Sometimes people think I'm stuck-up because I'm so quiet, but the truth is that I'm really shy and it's hard for me to talk to guys. I'm different with my girlfriends because we've been friends for so long and I feel more comfortable just being myself with them. But I feel like guys will laugh at me or reject me or ignore me.

Well, one day, I just made myself crawl out of my shell and I smiled at my crush. And he smiled back at me and said, "hi." So that gave me a little confidence to ask him a question when I saw him the next day—something like, "Did you think last night's homework was hard?" Then he waited for me after class because he didn't write down an assignment and asked me for it. We ended up walking down the hall together to lunch, which became a routine.

Conversation Pieces: Make Him Feel Like You Think He's Special

Don't you like to feel special? Guys are no different. Show a *genuine interest* in him as a person and the least you will be is "friends." The *most*? You get a boyfriend! (That's what happened to Sarah.)

Sarah wanted to talk to her crush about more things than just their math class, but she didn't know what to say. Then she had the idea of making a list of questions to ask him. That way, if she felt tongue-tied, she'd be able to think of something to break the silence.

I would never admit this to anyone, except maybe my best friend, but I wrote down all these questions to ask him. Like:

- *"What sports are you into?"*
- *"Do you have any brothers or sisters?"*
- *"What kind of music are you into?"*
- *"Who are you friends with?"*
- *"Did you go to the Dave Matthews concert last week? I did and it was awesome!"*
- *"Did you see [a movie] yet?"*
- *"Do you have a job lined up for the summer?"*

Then if I saw him in the hall or at the beginning of class, I felt like I had something to say. I wanted to show that I was interested in him without being too direct. I mean, I wasn't going to ask him out or anything—I'm way too shy for that. My mom said that lots of girls just talk about themselves, but that guys like it when girls are interested in them—*so that's where I got this idea.*

You *Can* Call Him!

Sarah was too shy to ask her crush out, but sometimes she felt like talking to him after school. One night after dinner she started her math homework—and thought of a question she could ask him. She got up her nerve and called him.

My heart was in my throat. I had that nervous feeling in my stomach. I kept telling myself, "you're excited, you're not a moron, you can do this!" And I did. I took three deep breaths and I called his number. He actually answered! I asked him the homework question and we stayed on the phone for an hour. After that we started calling and instant messaging each other at night. We became friends and then we started going out. We don't go out on actual "dates" because no one does that at our school. We just hang out all the time. No one is more surprised than me!

Gracie

"I love him, but was I ready? I was so mixed up."

Gracie just turned 17 and is a junior in high school. She has a brother who's 10 years older and married already. That leaves Gracie home alone with her parents, and she feels like an "only child." Gracie's mom is a gynecologist and talks about sex all the time, which embarrasses Gracie tremendously. She's more comfortable talking to her friends about personal issues.

Gracie has had a serious boyfriend since the beginning of freshman year. Last year, Gracie's boyfriend changed schools because his family moved to a nearby suburb. At first Gracie thought they should break up because they weren't at the same school. But she really loves him and he feels the same about her so they decided to stay together.

The saying, "Absence makes the heart grow fonder," is true for us. When we see each other, which is usually only on weekends, everything's great. We just hang out at one of our houses—usually his house since I have a car—and watch a movie most of the time. We talk every night. Everyone says we're too young to be so serious, but I don't know what "too young" means. We're really happy together.

And now there's the question of sex.

We've gone pretty far, but we haven't actually done it. Now he wants more. I'm not sure if I'm ready but I love him. This is a big problem for me now, and it's what I think about 99 percent of the time.

Gracie's dilemma—whether or not to have intercourse with her boyfriend—is a common dilemma that many of her friends have faced. A couple of her friends have regular sex with their boyfriends. They're monogamous, use protection, and have no problem with it.

But one of her friends had intercourse with her boyfriend of six months and he broke up with her three weeks later. Now she regrets her decision to "do it" with a boy who turned out to be a jerk.

I don't think my boyfriend's a jerk, but to be honest, if we get married it will be in a long time, after college. So the question is, do I want to give my virginity to him? That sounds weird, but that's how I think about it. I want my first experience to be special, and I love him, and I think it would be OK. But it feels like such a big step. Am I really ready for this?

Here's how Gracie dealt with the sex question.

The "P" Word—Protection

Gracie had sat through enough health classes to know that responsible sex is key. She knew to use a condom for protection from sexually transmitted diseases (STDs) such as herpes and AIDS; she also knew that condoms don't always prevent pregnancies. So her first question to herself—and her boyfriend—was how would they protect themselves?

My boyfriend told me that he'd use a condom, which was good, but I was scared that it might break and I'd get pregnant. That would be devastating

because I don't know if I could get an abortion,
although I am pro-choice. And my parents would die!
They'd think I was so stupid and irresponsible. So my
main issue was how not to get pregnant.

My school has a student health center where you
can get birth control without your parents knowing. I
just didn't want my mom to know, even though she's
a doctor. I went and got on birth control pills, but
even after that I still didn't know if I was ready.

Listing Pros and Cons

Gracie is a big list person—she has to-do lists, lists of
things she wants to buy, and priority lists for homework that she marks with a blue highlighter in her
assignment notebook. Since she was so torn about
whether or not to have intercourse, she decided to
make a pro and con list.

A lot of my friends are so much more impulsive
than me. They like a guy and they don't ponder
about these things—they just sleep with him. That's
fine for them but I'm much more "anal." I had to
explore the pros and cons before I could make a final
decision.

So Gracie made her list. The pros were:

1. I love him.
2. It would feel good.
3. Our relationship would be special forever.
4. We've done everything else so why not?

5. I trust him—I know he wouldn't cheat on me.
6. We've been together for almost three years.
7. I'm not planning on being a virgin until I get married anyway.
8. It's normal for girls my age who have serious boyfriends, at least at my school.

The cons:

1. It's a little scary.
2. My parents would be mad if they found out.
3. What if we don't get married and I regret it?
4. Even with a condom and birth control pills, there's a small chance that I could get pregnant.

My list helped me to make my decision. I decided to have intercourse with my boyfriend. I think my list helped me feel that I was making an informed and a responsible decision. I hope I don't regret it when I get older, but this feels like the right decision for me.

Emma

"I felt a lot of pressure but it didn't feel right."

Emma is 15 and just made the transition from a public middle school to a private high school. At first she didn't really know anybody at her new school, but the kids were pretty friendly so she's made a few friends. Emma has a baby sister who's almost four. Emma gets along OK with her dad but fights a lot with her mom.

Emma is really pretty. She will be the first to tell you that being attractive has its drawbacks as well as its advantages.

People say they envy me for my looks, but it's basically because of my genetics. I look like my mother's side of the family. They're from Spain, France, and Brazil. I have what people consider a pretty face and people always call me "exotic looking." But most of the girls in my middle school hated me and the guys did too. Lots of kids said mean things about me, like I'm conceited and impressed with myself. That's not true at all. They'd call me fat too because I was a little overweight. That's one of the main reasons I wanted to go to a new school—those kids were so mean to me.

Emma met a boy a few months ago that she really likes. He's in her French class and they've been together at parties. She's hooked up with him—just kissing, nothing more—a few times. But now he's asking her to give him oral sex.

Tim's awesome but I feel so confused. I'm not very experienced sexually—I had a boyfriend in seventh grade but it only lasted three weeks and all we didn't really do anything. This all seems so rushed. My friends tell me I'm uptight and if he wants me to do it, I should. I know a lot of girls who have oral sex with guys—one of my friends went to a party where all the girls gave all the boys oral sex. I think that's disgusting and degrading, and I wonder, if I give in to Tim, will I feel disgusted with myself?

I am very attracted to Tim and I fantasize about having sex with him but I know I'm not ready for anything like that. Plus, what if he dumps me like that other jerk? I would never get over that, ever. It would just crush me. At parties he gets mad when I talk to other boys but then he flirts all the time with other girls. It's like a double standard and it makes me not trust him. It doesn't seem right and it doesn't seem normal.

One of my friends, Jan, had a bad experience in this department. She had a boyfriend and after a few months he forced her to have oral sex with him. He said he'd break up with her if she didn't do what he wanted. So she did it, and he broke up with her anyway. He told all his friends that she was a "ho." He broke her heart. She was depressed for months. I'm not even sure she's over it yet. She told me not to do it. I'm so confused.

Emma was aware that she needed time to decide what she was comfortable doing with Tim. How would she feel about herself? Was this a real romance? Was it just a "friendship with benefits"? If he really liked her, wouldn't he like her even if she didn't give him oral sex?

Here's how Emma handled Tim's demands.

Q and A

Emma asked herself three questions that led her out of the labyrinth of her confused feelings. They were:

1. "What would it cost me to have oral sex with Tim?"
2. "Would I be doing it for my own pleasure or just his?"
3. "If other people found out, how would I feel?"

I decided that if I had oral sex with Tim, it would cost me my identity. I'd stop being me and change my values to be someone he wanted me to be, not someone I am.

I decided that oral sex is for guys, not girls. It wouldn't please me at all to do this because I think it's gross.

If people found out and called me a "ho" like they did to Jan, I would want to crawl into a hole and die. I would be mad at myself for doing something I didn't want to do in the first place and then getting blamed for it.

Thinking About Pro-Emma Behavior

Emma came to the conclusion that if she had oral sex with Tim and didn't get any pleasure from it, the behavior wouldn't be pro-Emma.

Pro-Emma behavior is positive behavior. It's behavior that makes myself—my thoughts and feelings—*as important as anybody else's. After a year in therapy, I know I am entitled to act in my own self-interest. And that would be to slow things down with Tim. If he doesn't like me anymore I'll be sad, but I know that it would be in my best interest to move on.*

You've probably guessed right—Emma said no to Tim. And she lost him. But she kept her values, her self-respect, and her power.

Summing It Up

So the subject of guys is complicated.

Sometimes you can't find right or wrong answers. Sometimes you just have to learn from experiences— be determined to learn from them. And even if things don't work out with a guy you like, you will always have another chance. That's *for sure.*

Are you the shy type? Chances are your crush is shy too. So think of ways to engage him in eye contact and conversation, like Sarah. Sometimes guys need a road map. They want to get to the destination (you) but they need directions on how to get there. Help him get to know you so that romance has a chance to bloom.

Do you want a boyfriend but not the heavy sexual stuff? Don't be afraid to be *yourself.* Use Emma's Q and A as a springboard for your own questions. Do love and sex go hand in hand for you, as they do for many girls (and less often for boys)? How would having sex affect life as you know it? Don't let a boy force you to do what you don't want to do.

Use Emma's pro-Emma behavior idea to develop *pro-you* behavior. Novelist Erica Jong says, "Pleasure is about power . . . a person who enjoys sex feels powerful," not submissive. Seize your own power. If you have sex, you should enjoy it and feel comfortable. Don't be afraid to say "no" if that's what feels right to *you*.

Are you in a serious relationship and feel ready to have sex with your boyfriend? Be smart like Gracie. Make sure you and your boyfriend are monogamous and protected. (If your school doesn't have a student health center like Gracie's, you can get birth control through Planned Parenthood or your doctor confidentially.) Make sure the pros outweigh the cons. Think about whether or not you are ready for the deepened intimacy that sex will bring to your relationship. Know that a trusting, loving relationship is a blessing and a responsibility. It requires hard work to keep it growing, like a garden.

Guys can bring fun and excitement—and heartbreak and frustration—into your life. The heartbreaks are hard, but don't give them the power to destroy you. Heartbreaks happen to *everyone* and you'll feel empowered when you realize you've survived. (Sometimes it's not even personal—a guy may not be mature enough for a relationship.)

Remember, you probably haven't met your life partner yet. Right now, and for years to come, it's all just practice. When the time is right, you *will* meet the right guy for *you*.

As Sarah says, "When I decided that I wanted to talk to my crush, well it felt like I was taking the hugest risk. But guys are fun. Or at least they can be. I'd say it was worth it."

Not "Just Saying 'No'"

Smoking, Drinking, Drugs

*I*f you can "just say 'no'" to cigarettes, alcohol, or drugs—and if your friends don't smoke, drink, or snort—consider yourself lucky.

But if you're like many girls, it's not so easy. Are these familiar thoughts?

- "The health-risk statistics don't faze me; I know lots of people who smoke and drink and swallow illegal substances—and they don't have tumors or liver disease or a fried brain."
- "Cigarettes, alcohol, and drugs are easy to get so why not try them? Everybody else I know does."

91

- "No one I know has died in a car accident because a driver was drunk."
- "Drinking some beers at a party loosens me up from my natural state of shyness."
- "My parents are hypocrites if they tell me not to smoke or drink. My mom smokes a pack a day because she says it helps curb her appetite—so why can't I? My dad said he tried marijuana when he was young and thinks it should be legal anyway. The first thing my dad does when he gets home is pour himself a glass of wine or grab a beer. So what's the big deal?"

In fact, you might feel uncomfortable about *not* trying something. You might be at a friend's house and she lights up a cigarette and asks if you want one. Or she's pouring some vodka or taking a hit off a joint, asking if you want to share. These are really hard situations. On one hand, you may be curious and in the mood for a little risk. On the other hand, you've heard time and again that smoking, drinking, and drugs are bad for you and can lead to a lot of problems. So what do you do?

Here are 13 questions to ask yourself. The answers are not simple.

1. Is your smoking (drinking, drug use) interfering with the relationships in your life? For example, do your clothes stink from

cigarettes so that your sister won't let you borrow hers? Does your boyfriend get upset when you get drunk at parties because you hook up with other guys?

2. Do you lie a lot to your parents about smoking, drinking, or drug use?
3. Do your friends tell you they're worried about you?
4. Have any teachers or coaches told you that you seem withdrawn or unmotivated?
5. Are you able to function in your normal, everyday activities? Is schoolwork up to par?
6. How's your energy level? Are you able to perform in sports as well as ever? If you have a job, do you do it energetically?
7. After drinking or using drugs, do you wake up in the morning with a headache?
8. Can you breathe easily? Does your chest hurt first thing in the morning or after a strenuous gym class?
9. Are you having problems with your short-term memory. For example, did you ever wake up after a night of partying and forget what you did the night before? Or, is it hard to retrieve information that you "know you know."
10. Have you ever passed out at a party?
11. Do you feel hooked? Can you *not even imagine* yourself without a cigarette? Do you feel like you *have* to drink or use drugs

when you're at a party or even before you
go to school?

12. Do you ever drink or use drugs alone?
13. Does that little voice inside tell you that
    you're out of control?

Did you answer "yes" to any of the questions? If so,
are you scared you have a problem? Well, you
might—but remember, it's *never* too late to make
some better decisions for yourself.

This chapter isn't intended to convert you into a
substance-free person because the issues are not
moral. It's not whether or not you *can* use substances.
Of course you *can*. Chances are you have friends who
know where to buy cigarettes, where to get alcohol,
and who can sell you drugs at school. *Can* is not the
issue. The issue is what you *choose* to do.

Three things to think about as you make your
choices:

1. **Personal safety.** Are you in a safe situation? If you
   do choose to drink or use drugs, are you with
   friends who could help you if you get sick? Or are
   you with people you don't know—who could take
   advantage of you if you get drunk? Do you ever
   get into a car with a driver who has been drinking
   or using drugs? Are you contemplating using
   drugs that are considered dangerous or addictive
   (heroin, cocaine, Ecstasy, and so forth)?
2. **Self-respect.** Are you being respectful to yourself?

3. **Integrity and courage.** Do you have the guts to *be yourself* in spite of what your friends are doing? If you don't want to drink or smoke, are you fearless enough to admit it to yourself and to act according to your inner feelings?

It's definitely not as easy as "just saying 'no.'"

Here are the stories of how three girls struggle with the issues of self-respect, integrity, courage—and smoking, drinking, and drugs.

Sue

"I know it's bad for me but I'm hooked."

Sue is 15 and goes to an all-girls parochial high school. She has three older sisters and a younger brother. Sue could be described as an "all-American girl." She plays goalie on her soccer team, gets good grades, makes good money baby-sitting, marches with her church youth group in the 4th of July parade. Sue just won first prize for her essay on Dr. Martin Luther King, Jr., in her school's Black History Month essay contest.

Sue has been smoking cigarettes since she was 13.

First I stole a couple of my mom's cigarettes. She never said anything about it. Then I talked my older sister into buying me a pack. One pack turned into half a pack a day. I was hooked after about a month. And I didn't even like smoking at first. I thought it was gross. It hurt my lungs. But I thought it was cool too. Lots of models smoke. Most of my friends do too.

Sue is trying to quit smoking for two reasons. First, she gets out of breath easily when she plays hard in a soccer game. Second, her boyfriend says she smells like an ashtray.

That really hurt my feelings, but he was just being honest. And once we went cross-country skiing and I couldn't keep up with him. It felt like someone was standing on my chest. That's what it feels like in soccer games sometimes.

But quitting cigarettes scares me. I'm so used to it and I can't imagine not smoking when I get up, after lunch, and when I get home from school. But my boyfriend really motivated me to quit because I want to smell nice. And I want to be a better athlete. So I'm trying, one day at a time.

Behavioral research tells us that you can't just quit a habit. You have to *replace* it with a new habit. After many repetitions, the new habit becomes ingrained as *your* habit. And since nicotine only stays in your system a few weeks, you're not *physically* addicted for very long.

Sound easy? It's not. But it is possible to quit smoking, and Sue is in the process of doing just that.

Sue's Antismoking New Habit Campaign has been helping so far.

Walking the Dog

This is a simple idea but it really can be effective. Sue takes long walks with her dog, Cocoa, to get her mind off smoking and to release the nervous tension she feels when she wants a cigarette. Research shows that regular exercise helps people stop smoking because it releases endorphins in the brain, which make us feel more relaxed and calm. So instead of relying on nicotine, Sue is trying to rely on her walks with Cocoa as a feel-good activity.

I'm glad I have Cocoa. I have to really make myself walk her but it can really help. Once, I wanted a cigarette so bad but I ran her twice around the block instead. I was so tired after that that I lost my nicotine urge. On weekends I must take her on 10 walks a day, but it really helps to get out instead of smoke.

Busy Hands, Busy Mouth

Smoking is a hand to mouth activity, so Sue thought it made sense to replace it with new hand to mouth activities. And she's had some success.

Chewing gum, hard candy—that's the kind of stuff I try to put in my mouth now instead of cigarettes. My boyfriend even gave me a new name for them—cancer sticks. So instead of cancer sticks, I have a stash of bubble gum, breath mints, lollipops—

*I especially like butterscotch hard candy. I'm
extreme—I must go through five packs of gum a day.
But it's better than the cigarettes. Drinking lots of
water helps too. My doctor said it washes the nicotine
out of your system faster. Another thing that keeps
my hands busy is playing with a rubber band. I twirl
it around with my fingers. I don't know why this
helps but it does.*

Gifts for Good Days

Sue figured out that she spends around $30.00 a week
on cigarettes. That's $120.00 a month—$1,440.00 a
year! So she felt totally justified in buying herself little gifts after smoke-free days and weeks.

*A new T-shirt, a new nail polish—even a
manicure. There are so many good things that the
money could go for. Actually, I started buying myself
a bunch of flowers every week that I don't smoke.
They're pretty—they remind me I don't want to stink!*

*I know this is in retrospect, but if someone had
told me how addicted I'd be, I don't know if I would
have even started smoking. My doctor said cigarettes
are as addictive as heroin. Can you believe that? She
also told me that my lungs were black. I've only been
smoking for two years. I was shocked.*

Sue's Antismoking Affirmation

Sue thought about why she wants to quit smoking cigarettes. She came up with these reasons:

"I want to smell good."

"I want to have more money for clothes, CDs, etc."

"I want my chest to stop hurting."

"I want to be healthy and be the best athlete I can be."

Sue made up an affirmation based on these ideas. She repeats these words to herself when she's lying in bed before sleep, and then again in the morning before she gets out of bed:

"Smoking is a money pit.
Cigarettes stink.
I want to be happy and healthy.
I will not smoke!"

My affirmation keeps me focused on not smoking. Every time I say it, it ingrains in my brain the whole point of stopping. My affirmation helps motivate me.

I'm proud of myself. I thought about getting a patch to stop smoking, but I think that's weird, wearing a patch around. And I knew I couldn't just cut down; I'd just cut back up again. So I'm going "cold turkey."

I haven't had a cigarette in 12 weeks. It's hard, but every week it gets a little easier. Actually I cheated one time but I just got back on track. Last Sunday, I made my room a smoke-free environment. No one can smoke in my room, not even my mom!

Meredy

"I got so drunk I scared myself."

Meredy is 16 and the youngest of three. Both her parents work and she has a lot of responsibility at home. She and her brother and sister have to help out around the house and go grocery shopping twice a week. Meredy is interested in saving endangered animals. She volunteered at a wildlife sanctuary for a biology project last year and really liked it.

For the past year and a half, Meredy's been getting drunk at parties every weekend.

I drink too much at parties. Everyone plays drinking games and I get so drunk. I don't remember what I did. My girlfriend told me I was kissing this guy—he wasn't my boyfriend or anything—and I don't even remember it.

Last Saturday night I threw up when I got home, and I threw up all day on Sunday. My parents made me go to church and I had to go to the bathroom five times during the service to throw up. My parents were mad at first, but then they made a joke of it. I was going to the library last night and my dad said, kidding, "Now don't drink."

I don't drink during the week, so I don't think I have a problem. But when I'm drunk, I do things I'd never do sober, like hooking up with boys I don't even know and being loud and obnoxious. People think I'm slutty, but I'm not. That's why I want to control myself. I've even thought of giving up drinking altogether but I think that's unrealistic because everyone drinks.

Meredy talked with a friend about her mixed feelings about drinking—but she found unsympathetic ears.

She said that if I stopped getting drunk, I wouldn't have any fun. She said no one would think I was any fun. I was afraid that I would lose all my friends if I stopped.

Here's how Meredy is trying to deal with drinking.

Family History 101

Meredy didn't think she had a problem with alcohol, but two uncles on her mother's side struggle with alcoholism—one is constantly in and out of rehab. Her paternal grandmother drank whisky all day. No one ever called her an alcoholic, but she died a few years ago of liver problems and colon cancer—both possibly related to her heavy drinking. So Meredy had to take a hard look at the possibility that alcoholism runs in her family and could affect her too.

Neither of my parents drinks so I didn't think we had a history of alcoholism. But when my mom and dad were talking about my uncle being back in rehab, it got me thinking about that. I still don't think I'm an alcoholic, but I also don't want to join the club of family alcoholics. That's one thing I don't want to sign up for. So this gave me a different kind of reason to think about staying in control.

Mindful Drinking

Meredy decided *to pay attention* to her drinking. She learned that most of the time, she keeps drinking even after she's drunk. With some mindfulness, she's learned to *moderate* her drinking. She's more *in control* now.

Most people stop drinking when they start to feel light-headed but I didn't. That's when I was just starting. So now, when I get that giddy, tipsy feeling, I know it's time to stop. For me, that only takes a drink or two. Then I'll pour myself some soda and drink that for the rest of the night. My friends are so drunk they don't really care. And I'm trying to stay away from drinking games. I say to my friends, "it's cool if you do it, but I got really sick once and I can't do it anymore."

Designated Driver—DD

Meredy regularly volunteers to be the designated driver (DD) for her group. This makes it socially acceptable for her not to drink.

One of my friends got in a lot of trouble. He was drunk and let someone else drive his car, but that person had been drinking too and the police stopped them. They ran a stop sign and almost hit another car. It was a big deal. So we all decided to have designated drivers. Unfortunately it took a near accident for us to take that very seriously.

I'm happy to be the designated driver. It gets me off the hook and when people tease me about not drinking I just say "I'm the DD."

I just had to be honest with myself. I knew I was drinking too much and I didn't want to be an alcoholic like my uncles and my grandma. I know I have to be careful. I still have a beer once in a while, but it's not every weekend and I'm definitely not out of control. And no one calls me a slut anymore.

Sarine

"I was definitely a pothead. But I stopped."

Sarine is 15. She hates sports and feels this is because her 16-year-old sister is a state champion diver. She loves her stagehand class, but aside from that she isn't too interested in school. She gets Bs and Cs and her parents tell her she should be getting straight As, just like her sister.

Sarine describes her family life as "less than healthy." Her parents are wealthy and travel a lot, leaving her and her sister with a housekeeper who doesn't speak English very well.

When her parents are in town, the stress level is high. They go to charity events three nights a week and are always busy getting ready to go somewhere.

Sarine's father, a lawyer, works 70 to 80 hours a week. When Sarine sees him on Sundays, he's usually in a bad mood and yells a lot. Sarine's mother is a Harvard law school graduate who has never practiced law. She serves on five volunteer boards and appearances are important to her—she spends $50,000 a year on her wardrobe alone. Sarine's parents put a lot of pressure on her and her sister to look perfect, act perfect, and, in general, be perfect people.

Needless to say, I fall short. I'm a little over-weight by my mom's standards, and of course I don't study that hard so my grades aren't great. But it's just too much. They ought to get a life and stop pressuring me to be somebody I'm not.

Before she quit, a few months ago, Sarine had been smoking pot regularly for around a year. She smoked almost every day after school. She was afraid that she was mentally addicted—she couldn't imagine a day without pot.

First I started just hanging out with kids who smoke pot. I was too scared to try it myself—I just wanted to watch, to see what it was like. Then at some point I tried some. It made me relax and not worry about anything. Believe me, this felt good to me. And since no one's ever home at my house, we just smoked in my bedroom. We aired it out and my parents were clueless. We did this practically every day.

I've gone to parties—and had parties—where kids do 'shrooms, Ecstasy, LSD, cocaine, and even heroin. I'm not into that although I have tried 'shrooms but it scared me because I felt really out of control. I didn't think pot was bad but I heard that it can give you cancer and it's worse than cigarettes because there's no filter. My aunt died of lung cancer and she suffered a lot so I did think about that.

The main thing that I worried about was that I didn't know how to stop. I sort of wanted to and I sort of didn't. My short-term memory was shot. I mean, it was hard for me to remember things on tests and stuff. That scared me. And I knew I would feel better about myself if I quit. But smoking after school was like a social ritual.

One day Sarine's sister was looking for a sweater in Sarine's closet—and found a baggie filled with pot. She told Sarine to stop or she'd tell their parents and they'd put her in rehab. Needless to say, Sarine was mad—but her sister may have saved her life.

My sister was scared for me. I really didn't want her to tell our parents but I wasn't sure if I could stop. I told her I'd try to do it on my own, but if I couldn't she could tell them and I guess I'd have to go to a treatment program or something. We had a really good talk, me and my sister, and I realized somehow that I had to stop the pot. The funny thing is that my parents did eventually find out—but that didn't turn out to be a bad thing. I just knew inside that what I was doing wasn't cool.

Here are **Sarine's Solutions** that helped her kick her pot problem.

Hot Line for Help

Sarine's sister has a friend whose mom is a substance abuse counselor, so Sarine asked this woman what a "friend" should do if she thinks she might have a problem. The answer: call the hot line—a free service—at the local hospital to check out the resources.

Sarine was understandably scared to do this and had her sister make the initial call. But the result was life changing. It was the first step in Sarine being in control of pot instead of the other way around.

I owe a lot to my sister. She called and set up a time for me to meet with a counselor. It was all confidential so I didn't have to worry about my parents finding out. She went with me to that first session.

After Sarine talked with the counselor a few times, she realized that she had to tell her parents. This was for two reasons. First, the clinic had to charge a fee based on her parents' income and she couldn't pay it.

Second, there was a legal issue: since she was under 18, they *had* to be notified at some point. This actually turned out to be a good thing, even though Sarine didn't think it would be at the time.

My counselor said that if I was being physically or sexually abused, they could make me a ward of the state, which means they would take me away from my parents and then my parents wouldn't have to know about the pot. But I'm not abused and I wanted to live at home with my parents. So the counselor said that I could tell them or she could call them and tell them or I could bring them in and we could tell them together. I told her I would tell them but that I also wanted them to meet her so we could all talk about it. I wanted her to tell my parents that I'm a good kid, that I just made some bad decisions, as they say.

So when I told my mom, she said she had suspected it for months but didn't know what to say to me. My dad was mad at first—he said we could be sued for kids smoking here and stuff like that—but eventually he understood that I was trying to stop and he was supportive.

Now I go to weekly meetings with my counselor and my family and I meet once a month with her. I also go to a support group once a month. About five or six kids usually show up there—kids like me who got into drugs but are trying to quit and it helps to talk to other people going through something similar.

I think this experience has helped my family and me communicate better and we get along better. They understand now that I can't be perfect, that I can only be me.

I'm taking it one day at a time, but I haven't smoked in a long time and I don't plan on getting back into it again, ever. I want to go to college pot-free.

Friend Environment Protection Awareness

Webster's New World Dictionary's definition of *friend*: "an ally, supporter, or sympathizer."

Webster's New World Dictionary's definition of *environment*: "all the conditions surrounding and affecting the development of an organism."

Webster's New World Dictionary's definition of *organism*: "any living thing."

Sarine (a living thing) is affected by her allies, supporters, and sympathizers (friends). If her allies, supporters, and sympathizers smoke pot, this will affect her development and she will smoke pot too. If her allies, supporters, and sympathizers don't smoke pot, she'll be influenced to quit. Sarine couldn't stop smoking pot until she protected herself from her pot-smoking environment.

In other words, Sarine had to get new friends. This was not an easy concept for Sarine to agree with, but eventually she realized that if she was going to stop smoking pot and get on with her life, there wasn't really much of a choice.

This was so impossible. How could I just give up my friends? But I thought hard about it. My friends were cool people, but I think one reason they wanted me to smoke is so they'd have company when they were smoking. And a place to smoke—they sort of used me for my house.

I'm lucky—I was still friendly with some old friends from freshman year who aren't big into drugs. I was able to renew my friendships with them. And some of the kids in the support group—I hang out with one or two of them too.

I know if I was still hanging out with my friends who smoke—well, I think I'd probably be in a residential treatment program by now. I just told them that my parents found out, and that they made me quit and won't let anyone smoke at our house anymore.

Butterflies Calendar

Sarine had a creative idea that helped boost her self-esteem—which in turn helped her stay away from pot. She calls it her Butterflies Calendar, and as you can see it's fun to make and pretty too!

I love butterflies because to me they symbolize freedom and change—you know, metamorphosis and all that. So I thought about how I wanted to change, like from a caterpillar to a butterfly.

I got a big calendar and stickers of butterflies from the craft store. I found sheets of stickers, each one of a different kind of butterfly. I'm sure you could get them anywhere. So every day I go without smoking pot, I put a butterfly sticker on that day. I like to count them and see that they look so pretty. My calendar isn't perfect, but I have 30 butterfly stickers all in a row and I'm still going strong. Actually, they motivate me. I like to give myself a sticker at the end of the day. It makes me feel good about myself.

Summing It Up

Sue, Meredy, and Sarine each had habits that interfered with the quality of their lives. Sue's cigarette smoking interfered with her sports' performance and her relationship with her boyfriend. Meredy embarrassed herself at parties when she drank to excess, which was most of the time. Sarine was worried about her memory and the fact that she *had* to smoke pot every day.

Ask yourself: Do addictions run in my family? If they don't, it doesn't mean that you *won't* become addicted to drugs or alcohol—but if a close family member has or had an addiction, it's likely that you *could* develop one too.

Do you have a habit you'd like to break? First, think of the reasons you want to change your behavior. After you figure out why you want to change your behavior, give yourself an affirmation. Use Sue's antismoking affirmation as a model—but use your own words that spring from your own motivations. Your affirmation will help keep you focused on your goal.

Then think of replacement behaviors. Try Meredy's idea of drinking soda in a glass instead of alcohol. (Just be sure you keep track of your glass so no one can put anything weird in it.) Or offer to be the designated driver. Try chewing gum, sucking on hard candy, or walking your dog, like Sue. Any behavior that isn't self-destructive is a good replacement behavior, so explore the possibilities. You *might* have to change your friend environment to do this, like Sarine had to do. Hard? Of course—but new friends may be lifesavers to you in the long run.

Sometimes habits are hard to change by yourself. Need to talk to someone? Call a hospital help line, like Sarine, to get the number of a teen youth center. Or ask a parent or teacher or close family friend to help you find a counselor or support group.

Reward yourself. With the money you save from cigarettes, alcohol, or drugs, buy yourself something *special*, like Sue. Make yourself a sticker calendar or give yourself other small tokens of progress, like Sarine. Be GOOD to yourself!

Most of all, be proud of the fact that you're developing new habits that will serve you well in years to come. Be proud of yourself because it's really hard to be an individual. It takes strength and resolve to decide what's right for *you*.

As Meredy says, "I always think, there's time to do things right. There's time to do things different. Just because other people do things, I don't have to. And I always think, today is the first day of the rest of my life."

Fresh Air

Taking Back Your Overscheduled Life

Are you gasping for breath in a sea of commitments? Do you race around from one activity to another so fast that you barely have time to go to the bathroom? Do you eat your lunch during English? Is the concept of "leisure activities" incomprehensible to you? If you answered "yes" to any of these questions, you may be suffering from the number-two cause of stress for teenage girls: an overscheduled life. (Number one is school stress.) In other words, you, like millions of girls, may have *way too much to do*.

An overscheduled life starts out harmlessly enough. For example, your friends play tennis so you decide to take indoor lessons on Sundays. You've been playing soccer since kindergarten and you want to continue in high school so that you can get a scholarship to college—practice is four days a week, 5–8 P.M. Games are every Saturday morning, 9–11 A.M.

But then the pressure builds. You want to take guitar lessons—Mondays at 9 P.M. is the only time your teacher has open. You have to volunteer at a soup kitchen so that you can fulfill requirements for the National Honor Society—there go Wednesday nights, your only night off from soccer. You have to baby-sit weekends to make money for a class trip to France— there goes your weekend down time with friends. You promised your mom that you'd help her in the garden—so much for Saturday afternoons.

And then there's homework, which you manage to squeeze in late Sunday afternoons and school-night evenings after 10 P.M. This leaves little time for sleep— before your over scheduled life starts all over again in the morning. Does this sound all too familiar?

Are you plagued by the symptoms of an over-scheduled life—biting your nails, suffering from headaches or stomachaches, feeling irritable, experiencing muscular tension, drinking too much coffee to keep awake, feeling nervous and hyper (as a result of the caffeine), or never being able to carve out a smidgen of personal time?

Girls learn by example. And many girls learn to overload their schedules by observing some pretty important role models: their parents. When parents work hard all day, attend several volunteer meetings a week, do laundry (or pay bills or make phone calls for work) instead of relaxing at night, and coach their kids' sports teams after school and on weekends—in short, have no room to breathe themselves—they're giving their children some clear messages:

- Time to relax is not part of a productive life.
- It's normal for people to run around all day and night until they are exhausted and depleted.
- Relaxation is not part of self-care.

Not to dis' your parents—they're doing the best they know how to do. But in some families, running on empty is the norm. Renewing oneself with self-care and relaxation is seen as—well—wimpy and weak. You may even think you're being *selfish* if you take some time for yourself.

Schools are often of no help in teaching kids to cope with an overscheduled life. Stress-management courses should be mandatory in every school in America, but they're rarely offered. One freshman at a highly competitive midwestern high school said, "Our school has one week of stress management in health class—one week in four years. And the teachers use textbooks—no one takes it seriously."

It's no wonder you may have trouble when it comes to "chilling." If you're like most girls, you have a "knowledge deficit" when it comes to relaxing and taking care of yourself.

Well—who tells you how to relax? Who tells you that letting go of tension is good for your health and sense of well-being? Who tells you that taking time for mental and physical rest will make you *more productive, a better student,* and *more energetic*? Who tells you that relaxation is the *antidote* to the stress caused by an overscheduled life?

Chances are no one tells you these things, even when your life feels like it's running away from you, full speed.

Dr. Herbert Benson, a pioneer in the field of stress management and the author of *The Relaxation Response,* is a fierce advocate of relaxation. He says that when you take time to relax on a regular basis, the health benefits are *enormous*. Dr. Benson states, "Our bodies are engaged in a kind of tug-of-war, stress on one end of the rope and relaxation on the other. Given the amount of tension we experience every day . . . stress always [seems] to overcome relaxation. But regular . . . relaxation evens the teams."

Here are the stories of three girls and how they're trying to take back their overscheduled lives. See how they've managed to carve time out from their busy schedules *for themselves*. Try some of their ideas! Be imaginative! Use them as jumping points for your own ideas.

Slow down your life and *take care of yourself*. Be kind to yourself! With all the stress in your life, you *deserve* to relax. And the more ways you have to relax, the better. YOU'RE WORTH IT!!!

Andie

"I had to learn how to say 'no.'"

Andie is 16. She's got two older brothers and two younger sisters—she's a middle child. After she graduates high school, Andie wants to go to a big out-of-state university—but with five kids, her parents can only afford to send her to a community college. So Andie's working hard for good grades (and hopefully a scholarship), involved in all sorts of activities, and has regular baby-sitting jobs. In other words, she's doing all she can to ensure that she'll be able to go to the college of *her* choice.

Understandably, Andie's schedule is maxed out.

I have absolutely no time. My life is crazy. My life's a rat race, and I'm just a kid! I have either golf practice or dance team practice every day after school. On Sundays, I volunteer in church nursery school. Saturdays, I take piano lessons and voice lessons. I have baby-sitting jobs on Friday and Saturday nights and I need those because I'm saving money for college. Lots of times I stay up until two in the morning finishing homework. I barely have time for my friends. I feel like I'm a productive person, but my life is out-of-control busy and I'm unbelievably overwhelmed.

Here are some ways Andie found to help slow down her life.

The People-Pleaser Disease Cure: Learning How to Say "NO"

Andie always felt like she had to please everyone, all of the time. Saying "no" didn't fit in with this view of herself. She was so bad at saying "no," that she said "yes" to *everything*, which created an impossibly full plate for her every day.

I couldn't get the word no *out of my mouth, even when I knew I didn't have time for something or I really didn't want to do whatever it was. I was so afraid that people wouldn't like me. I was the kid who did everything at home and everything at school. But I was burning myself out bad. I was nervous all the time. I got headaches. I knew I had to start saying "no" sometimes. I didn't know how to.*

One day, Andie got up her nerve to say "no"—by necessity. If she didn't decline a baby-sitting job, she was afraid she'd get a D on a history paper, which was a real possibility since she had started it late.

A family asked me to baby-sit during the week, and I had my history final paper due on Friday and I knew that if I said "yes," I'd never get my paper done on time, or I would do a bad job. So I did it. I said "no," and I found someone else to baby-sit—my younger sister. She's 14 and had the time to do it. She was actually happy to make the money. Nothing bad happened. *The people weren't mad at me. It was a* major *experience for me. It was the first time I said "no" to anyone. And I've said "no" again to baby-*

sitting jobs other than my regular weekend jobs. It actually feels pretty good. It feels like I have some control over my time, like I have a choice.

Prioritizing the Priorities

Andie was involved in so many extracurricular activities that she felt like her energy was stretched as thin as tissue paper. So she made a priority to-do list—the only activities she kept on her list were the ones that were *important to her.*

At first I couldn't decide what things were most important. Everything seemed like a priority. I had a blank piece of notebook paper for a long time. But then I thought, what are the things I love doing? What are the things I need to do to get a good scholarship? What do I hate to do?

I decided that I love to dance and sing. So I put those things at the top of the list—dance club and singing lessons. I need to make money so I put babysitting under those. But did I need to work both weekend nights? I thought no, maybe I could work during the day or ask to get off earlier at night so I could hang out with my friends.

I'm getting bored with golf so I put golf team toward the bottom. I like taking care of the babies at church so I put that in the middle. I'm getting really frustrated with piano so I put that at the bottom. I've been taking lessons for five years and I'm really not that into it anymore. I'd rather work on my dancing and singing than take piano lessons.

I decided to drop golf and piano. I thought I should tell my baby-sitting families that I need to be off by 8 P.M. on either Friday or Saturday so I can have a social life. That still leaves me with plenty of things to do. It leaves me time to be with my friends. I'm not an adult yet. Sometimes I want to just do things like hang out with my friends at the mall or go bowling.

Andie also wondered if she was overscheduling her life to please herself? To please her parents? Did she think she wouldn't get into college if she didn't have all those activities?

I think I was doing all that stuff because I see how busy my parents are with their jobs and working out and volunteer stuff—and I wanted to be like them. But it's too much for me. I decided to just do the extra things that I really love or that I really need to do, like baby-sit for college money. When I thought about what I actually enjoy doing and narrowed things down to that, I was really relieved.

The "To–Don't Do" List

After Andie made her priority to-do list, she had another idea on how to make her activity level more realistic and bearable. Her to-do list always seems to be on the brink of being too long. So Andie made a "to–don't do" list, which reminds her to try not to overschedule herself.

Andie's to–don't do list is universal. She doesn't change it from week to week, although she hopes to add to it periodically. So far, it has four things on it:

Andie's To–Don't Do List
- Don't say "yes" when it wouldn't be taking care of myself.
- Don't schedule extracurricular activities later than 9 P.M. more than twice a week. That includes school committees, volunteer stuff, lessons, study groups, and so forth.
- Don't do anything that would take away from schoolwork.
- If I add to my activity list, I have to subtract or modify something too.

Now I feel like I actually have a life. I'm still busy, but it's a good busy. I'm not as exhausted and overwhelmed like I was. Even though it's hard, I can say "no" sometimes. I can prioritize my activities, and I can use my to-do and to–don't do lists to stay focused. I'm really trying.

Cara

"I was so busy I never relaxed, ever."

Cara is 14 and will go to high school next year. She is her mom's only child, but since her parents are divorced and her dad is remarried, Cara has three half brothers, all under the age of 6. Cara loves her little brothers, but they've created one more role in her busy life: the instant baby-sitter.

Cara looks forward to summers when she gets to go away to camp in Michigan for two weeks. This is her last summer as a camper—next year she'll be a counselor in training. Cara is also ecstatic about taking a break from her overly scheduled life at home.

Cara's overwhelming schedule has less to do with *her* wants and needs and more to do with her *mom's* wants and needs. Her mother never finished college, and she wants Cara to have every advantage in life—including every kind of lesson imaginable.

At one point, I was taking horseback riding lessons, tennis lessons, ballet lessons, and played on a softball team—all during the school year, so I had homework on top of all that. It was crazy for me because I hated everything but the riding lessons. And it was crazy for my mom, because for one, she really couldn't afford it, and two, she had to drive me around for hours after school and on the weekends. I had the feeling I was doing this all for her, to make her feel proud of me. But I was so tired and unhappy. But I didn't know how to tell her.

Here's how Cara is trying to take back her life.

The Magazine and The Mom Talk

Cara wanted to talk to her mom but didn't want to hurt her feelings. Then she read a magazine with a teen advice column and found a letter that could have been written by her.

The girl was a year older than me and didn't know how to tell her parents that she didn't want to take piano lessons anymore. She thought they'd be mad. The advice, of course, was to try to explain her feelings to her parents and to try and negotiate a change.

So a few months before the end of school, I showed my mom the letter, and I said, "That's how I feel too, about all the things I have to do except for horseback riding."

Cara's mom was hurt at first but then she calmed down and talked with Cara. Cara's mom said she was just trying to give her things she never had. Instead of an argument, as Cara had anticipated, they had a good conversation and worked out a compromise.

My mom wants to "expose me" to all these things now so I can make a decision when I'm older about what I like and what I don't like. But we cut down the stuff. I don't take ballet anymore because I really hate it and the teacher tells some girls they have to lose weight and I hate that too. Instead, I'm taking the violin, which I've always wanted to do. But if I get too busy with school, my mom said I could quit. I'm also not going to play softball next year.

That leaves tennis and riding and violin. Tennis is OK—I don't really hate it—and I told my mom I'd try out for the tennis team in high school, which is fine—I want to join something in high school. And instead of taking riding lessons, which are expensive, I'm going to ride on weekends. I can volunteer to exercise some of the horses. I'm excited about that.

Showing my mom the letter in the magazine was a good thing to do. It helped me talk to her when I couldn't do it myself.

Meditation Rx

Cara has a friend whose mom is a meditation teacher. About six months ago, this friend had a birthday party sleepover, and her mom gave all the girls a How to Meditate lesson. Cara liked it a lot and now she meditates every day for 10 or 15 minutes.

Meditating is as easy as breathing. There's nothing to it, really. You just have to make the time, which in a way is giving yourself something else to do. But I look forward to it and I always feel good afterward.

Here are two ways Cara learned to meditate.

Word Meditation. Cara practices word meditation just before she goes to bed. (That's the only time she can find for regular meditation.) First, she sits on the floor with her back resting against her bed. She crosses her legs but you could sit with them straight out in front of you if that's more comfortable.

Then she closes her eyes and breathes in and out—through her nose—three or four times. She just tries to think about her breath going in and out of her body. She counts to three as she breathes in and she counts to three as she breathes out. The breaths should be deep, belly breaths.

Then you think of a word that calms you down. My word is soothe *but my friend's mom said it could be any word or image—my friend uses the image of a beach she was at in Hawaii.*

Cara silently says "soothe" to herself when she breathes in and again when she breathes out. She tries to focus her mind on her word. When she thinks of something that distracts her, which happens all the time, she just lets it pass through her mind and gets back to saying "soothe" to herself again.

I find that I have to always bring my mind back to my word but it gets easier the more I do it. My friend's mom calls the word a mantra, but that's a little too weird for me. I try to meditate for 15 minutes before bed. That's all there is to meditation.

Repetitive Movement Meditation. Any repetitive movement can be meditative—concentrating on an *activity* can work just as well as concentrating on a *word* to give you a mental break from the stress in your life.

Here are the activities that Cara finds relaxing and meditative.

Cara likes to **knit**.

My grandmother taught me how to knit when I was eight, and I picked it up again. Knitting is relaxing because it's the same motion, over and over again. I like to make scarves—I don't have to worry about shaping an armhole for a sweater or anything like that. I just knit and knit until it's long enough.

She also likes to **garden**.

I like gardening. I like digging in the dirt. I really like to do that. When I concentrate on digging up weeds or digging holes for flowers and planting them, I don't think about anything else. I just dig and grab weeds, over and over. Or dig and put a flower in the ground, over and over. I like how the dirt feels, and how the garden looks after I'm done digging around in it.

Puzzles also work.

I love working on puzzles. I like the ones with at least 1,000 pieces. I just sit at a card table and play around with my puzzle. First I try to find the border pieces and then I fill in the rest. If I have time, I can sit there for hours. I just think about the pieces in the puzzle—I don't think about homework or anything like that. It's great. It helps me get away from it all for a while. I like crossword puzzles too. And origami—it's like making puzzles out of paper—you fold paper in certain ways and make things like flowers and animals. I like that a lot.

All this meditation stuff makes me feel better. Maybe some people don't need to do this stuff, but I guess I have to say that I do. Or else I feel too cluttered in my head.

"My life was so out of balance."

Shelley is 15 and her nose is always in a book. She has an older brother who goes to a small private college in Boston. Her parents both have Ph.D.s and expect their kids to go to graduate school after college. In other words, Shelley has a smart, highly educated family and she feels pressure to follow suit. The whole family is active in their synagogue and most of Shelley's friends are from the synagogue's youth group.

My parents are amazing. My mom teaches at the university and has written five books on economics. She travels around the world giving lectures. My dad is dean of the college of arts and science and he's written a few books himself.

Shelley wants to live up to her parents' expectations for her. The only problem is that "free time" is virtually unheard of in her family. No one relaxes very much—there's always something that has to be done or somewhere to go.

Shelley started having physical symptoms that came from an overscheduled life—and that's when she *knew* she needed to do something in order to reduce her stress.

I started feeling really tense in my shoulders and neck. I had headaches all the time and my stomach was in knots. I found myself sighing a lot, which I learned is a sign of being stressed out. My jaws hurt and my dentist said I was grinding my teeth at night. He said it was because of stress. I felt like I just needed a week at a spa or something. I went to my doctor because my mom thought I might be sick and I was—sick of all the stress. I felt like I was drowning in the deep end of Obligation Lake.

Another sign to me that I was totally stressed was when I played The Circle Game. My friend presented it at a youth group meeting and we all played. She got it from a magazine. That game showed me that my life was definitely out of balance *and that I needed to learn how to chill.*

Want to see if your life is out of balance? Here's how you can play The Circle Game too.

The Circle Game
You'll need a compass, a piece of paper, a pencil, and a ruler.

Draw a big circle (using the compass) on the paper. Divide it into six equal sections (using the ruler). Label the sections school, health, family, friends, community service, and relaxation. Place a dot in each section that shows how happy and satisfied you are in that specific area—a dot near to the outer rim means you're very satisfied; a dot near the center of the circle means you're not very satisfied.

Now connect the dots. What do you see? Does your life look balanced? Or do the dots look out of balance and make a weird, asymmetrical shape? Do you feel happy about your friendships but not so good about your schoolwork? Do you do well in school but have no time for friends or community service? Do you eat pretty healthily but never make time to relax?

Shelley found that her life was sort of lopsided. She was very happy with her schoolwork, family, community service, and friends. But she was *very unhappy* about relaxation and health.

I didn't know how to relax, and I never exercised or even thought about my health. I just ate junk food to keep me awake at night so I could finish my homework.

The Circle Game helped me figure out that I needed to get some regular exercise and eat better. My mom's into fitness, so she helped me make a fitness plan. Now I try to exercise and eat better. And eventually I found some ways to relax too—which I call my stress-breakers.

Now Shelley finds that when she uses her stress-breakers, she's actually *more* productive when she gets back to her work. So here are **Shelley's Stress-Breakers**. And the list is long! See if any of them work for you!

Scheduled Study Breaks

Shelley used to stress herself out by studying for hours at a time with no break. She'd often stay up all night cramming for big tests, even though her dad told her that Harvard researchers have proved that it won't improve performance. Now she takes study breaks every hour and a half, gets a good night's sleep before tests, and *feels a lot better.*

I used to be crazy. I'd come home, study for 2 hours, eat dinner, and study for another 5 hours or more. Now I take breaks for 5 or 10 minutes. Sometimes I just look out my window at the scenery. Sometimes I get up and fix myself something to eat or drink. Sometimes I call a friend. Whatever I do, it's like my brain gets a little rest and I feel more refreshed. I also try to get to bed early before a big test. And my grades haven't gone down—if anything, they've improved.

Sweet-Smelling Candles

Shelley likes to light candles and put them around her bedroom. Last year she did a research paper on aromatherapy and learned that lavender's aroma actually makes brain waves longer so that you take deeper breaths and relax naturally. So her room is filled with the delicious smell of lavender.

My room smells really good. I love my candles. They have pure essential oils in them—synthetic oils smell the same but they don't have aromatherapy properties.

I use little votive candles and I put them in the holders with a little water on the bottom so they don't stick. My mom said it's OK as long as I don't leave the room with them burning.

The Color Blue

Research shows that when you see the color blue, your brain may release tranquilizer-like chemicals. Shelley used this idea to create a calm, tranquil environment in her bedroom. Her room is an oasis for her now—a replenishing space after an activity-laden, stressed-filled day.

I made my room into a retreat. It's pretty cool. First, I painted one of my walls baby blue. The rest of my walls are white so it looks cool. I don't hang anything on that wall except a picture I found in a National Geographic *magazine. It's a mountain lake and it reminds me of a lake we went to once on vacation.*

When I feel stressed out, like when I'm doing my homework and I know my next study break isn't for a while, I look at my wall for a few minutes and it gives me sort of a mental vacation.

Antistress Bath

Shelley uses this version of a bath concoction she found in one of her mom's fitness magazines.

> *2 cups Epsom salts—find at any drugstore*
> *1 cup baking soda*
> *2–3 drops of essential oils like lavender, frankin-*
>   *cense, or sandalwood (found at any health*
>   *food store)*
> *A few drops fresh rose petals (optional)*

Add the Epsom salts, baking soda, and essential oils to running *warm* water. (Hot water zaps your energy.) Throw in the rose petals for an extra treat. Relax for 20–30 minutes with a cup of tea and a magazine. Enjoy your time alone! Enjoy taking your space!

My bath is a stress-breaking ritual. I take one almost every night. I feel very relaxed after my bath. I feel like I'm in a better mood.

Saturday Night Home Spa

If she doesn't go out with her friends, Saturday nights are home spa nights for Shelley. Here are a couple of her home spa recipes. (Shelley saw them in a magazine, then made up her own recipes.)

Hair Smoothie

> *1 egg*
> *½ cup sunflower oil (you can get it at a grocery*
>   *store or health food store)*

¼ cup milk (whole milk or half-and-half works
   best)
4 tablespoons aloe vera gel (you can get it at a
   health food store)
4 fresh strawberries

Blend all ingredients in a blender. (You can also beat with a whisk or hand mixer.) Wash or rinse your hair, towel dry, and apply the smoothie—start at the top of your head and comb through to the ends. If you have one, put on a plastic shower cap. Leave smoothie on for 20–30 minutes, then shampoo out. Rinse well. Hair will be deeply conditioned and very shiny.

Sugar and Spice Facial

1 tablespoon sugar
½ teaspoon warm (not hot) water
¼ teaspoon apple cider vinegar
1 drop only cinnamon essential oil (get it at a
   health food store)
1 small bottle (6–8 ounces) sparkling water

Mix sugar with warm water in a small bowl. Add vinegar and cinnamon. Brush this mixture on a clean face with a cotton ball. Wait 5–10 minutes, and then dab sparkling water on face with a cotton ball until face is moist again. Allow to dry again. Repeat this process 2–3 times, until the sugar mixture sinks into the skin. There's no need to rinse.

The sugar dissolves dead skin cells. The cinnamon and vinegar keep skin clear and pores tight.

*I think it's fun to try new spa recipes. I find them
in magazines and some spas have websites so they
might have recipes there too. Sometimes my friends
sleep over and we give ourselves manicures,
pedicures, facials—you name it! We have a good
time. My home spa recipes are my most favorite
stress-beaters. It gives me something to look forward
to after a hard week.*

"Fave" CD Singing

Shelley belts out her stress with some of her favorite
CDs. This is not only stress-breaking—she loves to
sing and it feels really good to hit those high notes.

*I've always loved to sing. I just feel like singing
expresses my feelings and my spirit. Show tunes
really let you belt it out—My Fair Lady, Oliver!,
Oklahoma!, West Side Story, The Sound of Music,
Cats, Rent—anything, really. And I like pop music
too. I just close my door, turn up the music, and
SING!!!*

A Novel Idea: Book-Before-Bed Break

Shelley reads a lot for school, but it's rarely stuff that
she would read of her own volition. So for around 20
minutes before bed, Shelley reads a novel. Right now
she's into The Princess Diaries series, by Meg Cabot.

*I love getting lost in a good, juicy novel, and The
Princess Diaries series is my current favorite. I want
to read all the Princess books—there's* Princess in the

Spotlight *and* Princess in Love *too. I like biographies too. When I'm done with the three Princess Diaries books I'm going to read some biographies.*

I really feel like I'm giving myself a treat when I curl up in bed and read for a few minutes—that's all the time I have, but that's really all it takes.

Summing It Up

Andie, Cara, and Shelley are three totally different girls in three totally different situations—yet each suffered from an overscheduled life. And each girl found solutions to her stress.

Are you like Andie—are you a people pleaser who can't get the word *no* out of your mouth? Practice on a safe situation first—say "no" to people who you love and trust. Or say "no" when someone asks you to volunteer for something and explain your reasons. Tell him or her that it's nothing personal—you really don't have the *time* or *energy* to do whatever it is he or she wants you to do. Once you say "no" and it works for you, it will be easier to say "no" the next time you need to do so.

Are you maxed out with activities? Prioritize them—and cut some out, like Andie and Cara. Only keep the extracurricular things you *want* to do—and lose the rest. Your time is *valuable*. Don't waste your free time on things you hate!

Do you need stress-breaking activities, like Shelley, to put some balance into your life? This chapter is full of them. Try some. Meditate. Paint your walls blue. Create a home spa. Sing to show tunes. Read a juicy novel. Schedule study breaks. These are just a few good ideas—you can probably think of a gazillion more. Make your list go on and on. Add to it often.

It feels good to be productive, but remember: the harder you work, the more you need strategies and stress-breakers to balance—and take back—your over-scheduled life.

As Cara says, "I like being busy but I like my time to myself too. For the first time I see that it's important. I mean, I need to know how to relax too."

Picking up the Pieces

When Your Parents' Divorce Shatters Life as You Know It

Are your parents divorced? If so, you're not alone. Half of all marriages end in divorce. This means millions of girls have parents who aren't married anymore.

Everyone has serious, strong feelings when their parents split up. Divorce is a tragedy, and it's normal to have feelings of grief and mourning for years afterwards. Sometimes you may mask your feelings with hostile behavior that you—and your parents—may not quite understand. Sometimes you may hide your feelings. But too many times, a girl's feelings are seen as temporary and unimportant. You may feel like you don't have anyone to listen to your complaints about how the divorce affects *your* life.

Divorce can disrupt one of your major "jobs," which is separating from your family. Instead of separating in a gradual, natural way, divorce may inflict a sudden, unwanted distance from one parent. Divorce may also push you too close for comfort to a needy parent, forcing you to put *your* need for independence—a normal and healthy need!—on hold.

Researcher Judith Wallerstein has talked with hundreds of kids whose parents have divorced. Excluding violent and abusive families, Dr. Wallerstein found that kids are *always* unhappy about their parents' divorce, despite the common assumption that "when the parents are happier, the children are happier." Dr. Wallerstein also found—not surprisingly—that kids in divorced families are more likely to be overwhelmed by feelings like sadness, loneliness, anger, fear, and worry than children in non-divorced, intact families.

The list of hassles brought on by divorce is practically endless. Here are some common complaints:

1. You may all of a sudden have to cope with moving from the home you grew up in, which may mean changing schools and living far away from your friends.
2. You may not see one parent very often anymore. You may have a parent who moves away to a different state. Or you may have a

parent who doesn't see you consistently even if he or she still lives in the same city.

3. For the first time, you may see one or both of your parents cry in front of you.

4. Your parents may continue to feel hurt after the divorce and may try to "poison" you against the other parent. Your mom may say nasty things about your dad or vice versa.

5. Guilt: you may feel like the divorce was your fault or that if you were somehow "better," your parents would still love each other.

6. Your parents may put you in the middle of their relationship. Your dad may ask you questions about your mom's dating life, or your mom may ask you to give messages to your dad.

7. Your parents may use you as a shoulder to cry on. Your dad may sit down over coffee and talk to you as if you were his friend. Or, instead of having a social life of her own, your mom may want to be with you on Saturday nights. In both cases, you may feel uncomfortable because you'd rather be with your friends.

8. Your parents may be exhausted, depressed, overwhelmed, and emotionally unavailable to you and your siblings. You may have to take care of younger brothers and sisters because your parents have dropped the parenting ball.

9. One parent may pick on you because you resemble your other parent.
10. You may not like your parents' boyfriend/ girlfriend—or your new stepparents.
11. You may not get along with new stepsiblings.
12. You may have financial problems. Supporting two households can be a huge financial drain, even when both parents work. You may not be able to buy things that you never thought twice about buying before the divorce.

Because you're under a lot of stress, support from other people couldn't be more important. Think: loving grandparents, aunts or uncles, teachers, neighbors, friends' parents, youth group leaders, camp counselors, ministers or rabbis, therapists, and so on.

Your parents' divorce: hard to deal with? Sure.

Can you learn to cope with it? YES!

Here are the stories of how three girls cope with their parents' divorce.

Megann

"Am I the mother of the family now? Since my parents got divorced, it sure feels like it!"

Megann is 17 and a junior in high school. She has wavy dark hair and is tall—5 feet 9 inches and still growing. She loves to play tennis and finally made the tennis team after two years of trying out and not making it.

Megann's parents are wealthy. They've been divorced for one year, which took three years to finalize because of a war over money.

My dad is rich, but to be honest, it just made things worse. They fought about the house, the art, and the condo in Florida. It makes me feel sick inside because all they cared about at one point was money. How could they ruin our family? What about me and my little sister? Aren't we worth something?

Six months ago, Megann's mom went back to school. Once a "milk and cookies mom," she suddenly had little time or energy to spend in her role as a parent.

She's always wanted to be a teacher, so now she's back in college finishing her undergraduate degree. Then she wants to go to grad school. She's hardly ever home, which means I have to take care of my sister, who's nine. Our cleaning lady goes home at four, so I have to make dinner, help my sister with her homework, and clean up the kitchen because when my mom gets home, she's too tired. Twice a week I have to drive my sister to soccer practice. I don't like all this responsibility but I feel sorry for my sister. When I was her age, my mom was always home for me. If I didn't help out I'd feel really bad for her. It sucks.

Megann's dad lives in a nearby suburb. Though they were once extremely close, she thinks the divorce has put an emotional as well as physical distance between them. Megann wonders if she'll ever feel close to her dad again.

I'm expected to spend weekends with him, but it's hard because none of my stuff is at his condo. None of my friends lives near him. I can't live in two places at once, so I don't see him a lot. And I don't even think he cares that much. He travels a lot for his job so he's never home. And now he's got a girlfriend so he doesn't really want me sleeping over on weekends anyways.

I really don't trust that my dad cares about me that much. He buys me things, but we don't talk that much. He doesn't listen when we do. He basically ignores me. When something goes wrong, he has a way of always making it my fault. Once I got so mad at my dad because he just walked away when I was telling him about a math test. I kicked a hole into a door, I was so mad.

I still don't understand how my dad could leave his family. I take it very personally, even though he says the divorce doesn't have anything to do with me. I think that's bullshit. Of course it has to do with me. It makes me feel sad every day of my life.

Megann has a hard time looking up to her parents as role models. It's not easy for her to imagine herself in a successful, mature relationship because, after 20 years, her parents' marriage fell apart.

Growing up is incredibly scary. I can't imagine ever getting married—but I do want to meet the right person someday. I don't know if I'll ever have children. I don't want to screw them up the way my parents have screwed me up.

Megann's mom has a new boyfriend. He's 12 years her junior, which makes him only 11 years older than Megann. Her mom jokes about her "boy toy," but Megann feels uncomfortable about their age difference. Megann feels hurt and angry at her mom for spending so much time with her boyfriend. She acts out her anger by doing things her mom wouldn't want her to do.

My mom acts like a teenager since she met Bill. She's the one out having fun on weekends while I stay home and feel depressed because I'm lonely and I don't have a boyfriend. I've never had a boyfriend. She even chose to be with Bill instead of going to my piano recital. She doesn't even look like a mom anymore. She wears ridiculously short skirts and these low-cut tank tops. I feel left out of my mom's life and it hurts a lot because I try so hard to be good to her. I listen to her problems. It's like I'm her mom instead of the other way around. I'm homesick for my old mom. I feel like my new mom doesn't have any time for me.

Last Saturday night, when my mom was sleeping over at her boyfriend's place, some friends came over and we smoked weed. I'd never tried it before, but what the hell, no one's ever home anymore, no one would ever know, so why not? What do parents expect when they're not around to parent their kids? I don't even care if she finds out.

Megann was furious with both parents because she felt they had stopped nurturing her. She felt like the strings were cut too soon. So she "acted out" her feelings by kicking and smoking. The problem was that her behavior didn't change her situation or her feelings. Here's what *did* help.

Speaking up and Getting Real

Megann talked to her mother and father separately about her true feelings. Here's the list of problems she discussed with her mom:

- She told her mom that she's embarrassed about how young Bill is.
- She asked her mom to please not sleep over at Bill's house because it made her feel uncomfortable and unloved.
- She asked her mom to stop using her as a sounding board—that she was sick of hearing about her mom's problems with her dad.
- She also told her mom she hates being responsible for her sister.

Megann's mom was cool. First of all, she had no idea that Megann was feeling so bad. She apologized for being preoccupied with her own life. Before

Megann spoke up, her mom thought the family had adjusted well to the divorce. But she was *so* wrong.

Before I let it all out, my mom saw me as she needed to see me. Now she sees me as I am.

Megann's mom agreed to make some changes. She didn't promise perfection, but she did promise to try to be more sensitive to Megann's needs. She said she would stop sleeping over at Bill's. She promised to stop talking to Megann about Megann's dad. She arranged for carpools for her youngest daughter so that Megann wouldn't have to drive her to soccer practice. And she made a commitment to come home as soon as her classes were over, instead of stopping for coffee with classmates. That way, she'd be home for dinner most nights.

Here's what Megann discussed with her dad:

- She told him that if he wanted a relationship with her, he was going to have to help her figure out how and when they could see each other.
- She told him that she couldn't see him on school nights because she would feel disrupted from homework and activities. Weekends didn't work because she wanted to be with her friends.

He said he wanted to try to have a better relationship and asked if I'd like to get together for

Sunday dinners. I said "yes." It felt good that he wanted to make the effort to see me on a regular basis.

Megann is hopeful that the changes she has arranged with her parents will help her to get along with them better so that she feels better about her family.

I was sick and tired of the situation. I think talking to them about how I want things to be different definitely helped. I mean, we still have some problems, but things are a lot better than before.

Soothing Skills

Megann also developed some personal techniques to help soothe herself when she experiences sad and angry feelings.

It helps when I can do things to soothe myself. It doesn't make the divorce go away, but at least I'm trying to cope instead of letting everything get me down.

Megann keeps a journal.

I don't journal every day, but usually I write in it every week or so. I might write one sentence or five pages. Sometimes I draw pictures. Sometimes I copy down words to songs I like. Sometimes I write my opinions about things. Sometimes I write poems. My journal is very personal.

Megann plays the bongo drums to her favorite CDs.

This sounds weird but it really relaxes me. I put on music and just drum away. I imagine that I'm drumming all my bad feelings out of my mind. I feel physically drained after I play my bongos. But I feel better too. I like to drum to pop music, mostly.

Megann likes to talk with her piano teacher, Mrs. Wells.

My piano teacher is cool. I can talk to her— sometimes instead of a lesson, we just talk. Mrs. Wells's parents were divorced when she was around my age, so she really understands. She tells me I'm talented and smart and that I can make something of myself. So when I feel like I'm a total loser because my family's so screwed up, I think about what she said.

At one point, I considered staying home after I graduate and going to a community college because I wasn't sure I wanted to leave my family, but Mrs. Wells said, "No way. Go away to college. It will be the best thing for you." So I'm going to apply to schools on both coasts. I really needed someone to give me permission to leave this mess. I'll always be grateful to her.

Ali

"I have no control over my time."

Ali is 15. She's thoughtful, soft-spoken, and short with an athletic build. Ali has engaging blue eyes that look sad, even when she's smiling.

Ali's parents got divorced when she was two years old. Neither has remarried. Like Megann, Ali's parents live in close proximity, but that's where the similarities end. Instead of minimal parental involvement, Ali's parents are *overinvolved* in her life.

For the past 13 years, this has been Ali's schedule:

Monday through Thursday with her mom
Friday, Saturday, and Sunday with her dad
Christmas with her mom (she's Catholic)
Hanukkah with her dad (he's Jewish)
Easter with her mom
Passover with her dad
Every other spring vacation with her mom
Every other spring vacation with her dad
Summer vacation as follows:
> June and July with her dad (usually on a camping trip)
> August with her mom (usually visiting her grandparents in Seattle)

It's frustrating because my parents tell me where I have to be and when. I never have time to myself. I never get to spend summers with my friends, just hanging out at home. I had to plead with them to go downstate for a swim meet, because that meant that I'd miss a weekend with my dad. It's insane how they control my life. I love both my parents, but sometimes I feel like I live in a jail.

Ali has fantasies that her parents will reconcile someday. This is a normal feeling, but it's especially strong for Ali—after all, her parents seem to get along *so* well. And it really happened to a girl in her class.

My mom always asks me questions about my dad, and my dad asks me questions about my mom. So that means they still care about each other, right? I hope that they'll get back together. When I was four, I dreamed they got married again. I still have this dream sometimes.

Ali feels envious of her friends whose parents are married.

My best friend is so lucky. She has a happy family and they all live together. I love spending time with them. I wish I lived in a family like that. I don't even think she knows how lucky she is.
Once my best friend and her family invited me to go with them to Florida for spring break, but could I go? Of course not! My mom said "no" because it was her turn to have me, and she wouldn't give me up! They had so much fun in Florida. They went scuba

diving and it was sunny every day. Just thinking about what I've missed because my parents are divorced makes me want to cry.

Ali wishes her parents had taken *her* feelings into account when they decided to get divorced.

After all, I was only a baby. I couldn't even speak in sentences yet. Babies need both their parents living in the same house, even if they can't say it themselves. When I was five, I asked my mom why she doesn't live with my dad. She told me that they just grew apart. Well, why didn't they work harder on growing back together or something?

My parents don't seem to realize that their divorce is very inconvenient for me. It has made my life hell. Sometimes I need something that's at my mom's when I'm staying with my dad, and it's tough luck for me because he never has time to take me back to my mom's to get it. And my mom does the same thing. It feels like I don't have a real home. I'm always going to someone's house and leaving someone's house. I can never win.

Ali feels angry and hurt by her parents' divorce, but unlike Megann, she's never acted out her feelings because she's afraid of upsetting her parents. The last thing she wants to do is create more disruption in her already disrupted life. She holds her feelings inside herself.

I get so mad but I keep my feelings to myself. If I told my mom I was angry about having to spend spring vacation with her instead of going to Florida with my friend, she'd feel hurt. I couldn't handle that because I feel guilty enough about being such a burden to them. I've spent my whole childhood trying to adapt to their divorce, going back and forth, back and forth. And they think I've adapted so well. If they only knew!

When Ali holds her feelings in, she gets headaches and stomachaches. That's because feelings have to go somewhere; if they're not expressed, they can become somaticized, which means that they can wreak havoc on our bodies by causing physical symptoms. Ali understands this. She has worked hard to find ways to express herself in positive, constructive ways. Here's what she's discovered so far.

Art

My art helps me cope. It's my creative outlet. My best friend cooks to be creative. My mom writes. I paint. I like acrylics. Right now I'm into abstract. I just let myself go and the colors just flow out onto the paper. I also like to make collages. I cut pictures out of magazines and mount them on cardboard, then spray on shellac. Right now I'm making a collage of animals. I love my art. It's the only time I ever really feel free. When I grow up I want to be an artist.

A Three-Way "Heart to Heart"

It was awkward and scary, but we all sat down together and I told them a few things. First, I wanted to know the real reason they got divorced. Then I wanted to know if they think about getting back together, and if not, why neither of them has remarried after all this time. I also want them to agree that I can spend vacations any way I want to. At least I wanted a say-so.

Ali's mom and dad were open to negotiating the vacation issue. They agreed to try to be more flexible. They promised Ali that if she got invited to go somewhere over another spring break, she could go if they knew the family. They also agreed that they would each plan summer vacations *with* her instead of dictating the plans *to* her.

Ali's mom and dad each told their side of the divorce story. Each emphasized that they are good friends, but aren't interested in getting remarried. Her dad said that when they got married, they were "young and stupid." They were barely out of their teens and they couldn't handle the pressures of marriage. Ali's mom said that she wanted a career and her dad wanted a housewife. They had different dreams and different goals, and they get along better now than when they were married.

Ali told her parents that she always secretly hoped that they would get remarried like one of her friend's parents did—that it was hard to accept that this would never happen. Her dad put his arms around her and said, "Honey, you are the best daughter we could ever imagine. Don't ever forget that. Mom and I don't regret for one minute that we were married, because we got to have you. But our lives have moved on."

After he said that, I got kind of tearful but I felt that a huge knot was lifted out of my gut. I finally understood what I had been feeling for so long. I had been feeling guilty for being born, and if my parents got remarried I thought I wouldn't feel that way. But now I realize that it's OK, that we're a family anyway.

I feel a lot better about my relationship with my parents. I'm glad we had our heart to heart. It was important for me to let them know how I feel. I'm more open with them now, and they're giving me more choices. I'm a lot happier now.

Monique

"My father got remarried and it's changed everything for the worse."

Monique is 17. Bright and articulate, she is one of a handful of African-American students at a suburban high school. She has twin brothers, two years younger.

Monique's parents had been separated for three years before their divorce became final, two years ago.

One month later, Monique's father surprised her by marrying his childhood sweetheart while she was away at summer camp.

It was a surreal experience. I stepped off the bus, and I saw this woman with my father who I thought was a family friend. He said, "Monique, this is Clara, my new wife." I just stared at them in disbelief. I didn't know whether to laugh or cry. I was in shock.

My life used to be relatively simple and predictable. I lived with my mom and saw my father on weekends. My father would usually take me and my brothers out for dinner and to a movie, and sometimes we'd sleep at his house. It was like a bomb dropped on our life when he got remarried.

Monique feels sad that she doesn't see much of her father anymore.

He moved into Clara's house, 45 minutes away from us. I don't have my driver's license yet, and the bus takes two hours to get there. We don't see him on weekends anymore because my mom works on Saturdays and can't take us. And he won't come down to get us because he says his life is too hectic.

My father used to be such a big influence in my life. Now I hardly ever see him. It feels really bad. There's a huge hole in my life.

Monique doesn't like her stepmom.

My father wants us to go on vacation with him this Christmas, and that would be cool except that I can't stand my stepmom. I don't even like calling her a stepmom. I call her Clara. She has three little kids of her own and now they have a baby boy. My brothers and I feel like second-class citizens over there.

The last time I spent any time with them was last June, just after school was out. They were all in L.A. visiting Clara's mother, and I flew in all by myself because my brothers wouldn't go. It was a four-hour plane ride. It gave me the creeps, even though I'm obviously old enough to fly alone. But I always get afraid the plane's going to crash. Ha! That must be because I feel like my life's crashed!

I stayed for a week. The baby was sick so they spent most of their time taking care of him. Clara made me feel like I was in the way all the time. I swear she thought I was the one who got the baby sick. She wouldn't let me near him, and he's my half-brother. One morning I was starving and I took a yogurt from the fridge, and she yelled, "That's the baby's. Put it back." My dad was sitting right there, reading the paper. He didn't say anything. He didn't stick up for me.

When I got back, I told my brothers what happened. They said they totally understood. They said the reason they didn't want to go was that Clara's mean to them too. My one brother told me that Clara called him "stupid" because by accident he stepped on the baby's hand. Clara obviously hates us. Her kids are spoiled brats. I have no idea when I'll see my father again, really. I lost a lot of respect for him when he married that woman.

Monique worries about her mom.

Before my dad got married, everything was sort of balanced in my mind. They both were alone and they both were our parents. They went to all our school events together. They talked to each other when they had problems with us.

Now my mom's the only one who's alone. And now she's the only one who's raising us. She's a great mom. But what will she do when we're all away at college? Her family doesn't live near us. I worry about that. I worry that she'll be alone for the rest of her life.

Monique is worried that she won't be able to go to the college of her choice.

My father is a college professor. Last year he told me that he'd pay my tuition only if I go to his school. That's because he gets a huge discount. But I don't know if I want to go there. I'm number three in my class and I could get into lots of other schools. I always wanted to go to Harvard. But I honestly don't know how I'll ever be able to pay for that unless I get really good scholarships.

It hurts me so much. I always assumed that my dad would support me 100 percent in college because he's always said that he would. He's always been so proud of me. I know he saved money for us to go to college. But now he's got to pay for seven kids instead of just my brothers and me. So he's cutting corners on my education.

Monique feels rejected by her father. She wanted to talk to him and put their relationship on a better track, but he was always "too busy." She decided to call him up one day out of the blue. She asked him if he even wanted to spend more time with her. His answer: "I don't know right now."

That was an arrow right through my heart. I couldn't believe it. My own father. My mom told me that he has big problems and not to let him get the best of me, but that's impossible. I can't just let feelings like this go, like it doesn't matter. It matters a lot.

Here's how Monique copes with her deeply painful feelings.

A Letter

Monique wrote her father a letter telling him how he made her feel. She sent the letter by "snail mail" just before her 17th birthday. The letter didn't change her situation, but it did help her change how she felt inside. She felt like she had *expressed herself*.

I wrote 10 pages. I told him that if he ever wanted a relationship with me ever again, he'd have to prove that he could be a real father again. I toyed with the idea of not sending it, but I really wanted him to know my feelings. I remember when I finally addressed an envelope and put on the stamp. I held my breath while I dropped it in the mailbox. I thought to myself, "you can't change him, but you can take control of the situation." Mailing that letter was a big step for me.

Healthy Distractions

Monique gives her problems a rest by keeping busy.

I work on the school paper and I just joined the debate team. I'm never home before dinnertime on school nights, and sometimes I don't get home until after eight. I spend lots of time with my friends on weekends. I volunteer in the nursery at church. Being busy keeps my mind off my problems. I don't feel like I'm avoiding my problems—I just like to put them on hold sometimes.

Counseling

Monique goes to weekly therapy sessions.

I know that I need to talk about my feelings and that's why I go to therapy. Once a week I just let

*everything pour out. Talking about my feelings helps
me feel better. At first I felt guilty—like I should be
able to handle my feelings all by myself. But now I
don't feel like I have to be some kind of superhero.
The lady I talk to gives me advice sometimes, and
sometimes she listens and asks questions that lead
me in the right direction.*

Keeping Her Eyes on the Prize

Monique tries to stay in touch with her strong resolve
to succeed in life.

*I am determined not to let my parents' divorce
ruin my life. I plan to learn from my experience. I
plan to have a successful career, probably in law. I
plan to get married someday, but probably not for a
long time. And when I do, I'll never get divorced.
When I feel sad about my dad, I think about all this.
When I put my mind to something, I usually succeed.*

Summing It Up

Divorce is really hard on a family. It may be the hardest thing you've ever had to deal with—or will ever
have to deal with—in your life. Megann, Ali, and
Monique have experienced different divorce situations, but they've each found ways to cope with the
common pain of parents splitting up.

All three girls found that expressing their feelings
directly to their parents helped them feel better inside

and helped them feel more in control of their lives. This took courage with a capital C. It's not easy to bring up difficult feelings in most families, and it's especially hard when your parents are divorced because for a period of time, everyone usually feels overwhelmed, angry, helpless, and sad.

Megann and Ali found that talking directly to their parents helped ease their bad feelings. Initially, Megann acted out her feelings; Ali held them inside. Both girls realized that these behaviors were not helping them feel better. Both girls found that their parents responded pretty well to direct communication.

Monique wanted to talk with her father, but he just couldn't talk to her. Who knows why? Maybe he felt guilty, maybe he's not very mature, maybe he doesn't know how to express his feelings. One thing is for sure: he couldn't talk to her because of *his* limitations, not hers.

So Monique used a creative approach. She wrote her feelings down and sent them to him in a letter. She figured that this was the next best thing to talking with her father directly. She was *really* disappointed in him as a father—but she felt relieved and *empowered* by mailing the letter.

Another thing that helped Megann, Ali, and Monique was support from special people. The amount of support you need, especially in the first few years of the divorce, cannot be exaggerated. Reach out to people you trust. Megann has her piano teacher. Ali has her best friend. Monique has her therapist and she also developed deeper bonds with her brothers. Support from others can make all the difference in the world and can help you feel a lot less lonely.

Creative outlets are really important to Megann, Ali, and Monique. Think of creative outlets that *you* could pour yourself into. You could do something artistic, like Ali's painting and collages. If you like to write, try journaling like Megann, or join the school paper like Monique. Like to argue? Seriously—check out the debate team at school. And pounding on the bongos (or pots and pans if you are bongoless) to your favorite CDs, like Megann, requires absolutely no talent at all and feels really good! Creative outlets help soothe even the deepest, darkest feelings.

Megann, Ali, and Monique searched for solutions to hard feelings, and each girl has found some that work for her. You can too.

As Megann says, "I'm doing the best I can under the circumstances, at this moment in time. Divorce is hard, and I've been working hard, trying to figure things out. I deserve to feel proud of myself for that. And I really do."

Mr. Sandman,
Bring Me a Dream

Getting to Sleep When You Can't

*D*o you ever go to bed at a decent hour and end up just lying there, wide awake with your eyes closed, until your alarm goes off the next day? Do you ever toss and turn all night with a million different thoughts racing through your mind? Do you ever wake up in the middle of the night and have trouble getting back to sleep? Do you ever wake up in the morning feeling exhausted instead of refreshed?

Chances are you can answer "yes" to at least one of these questions. According to experts, more than 84 million Americans have experienced insomnia or problems sleeping through the night.

Insomnia can breed insomnia. For instance, you may dread going to bed because you're afraid that you'll stay up all night. This may become a self-fulfilling prophecy, which means you stay up all night worrying that you'll stay up all night. Or you might be tired and crabby the next day and take a nap after school—and feel awake, rested, and not at all sleepy when it's time to go to bed.

People get insomnia and lose precious sleep for lots of reasons. Here are just a few:

- You drank too much coffee or cola during the day and your mind is racing in a caffeine buzz at 1 A.M., even though your body is tired and begging for rest.
- Anxiety keeps you up at night, like worrying about a test or some dumb thing that happened at school.
- A too–late night snack gives you a late-night stomachache.
- You just got back from vacation and have jet lag.
- Your family is making lots of noise outside your bedroom.
- You feel jumpy and alert and agitated—your adrenaline's pumping—because you're anticipating something big the next day, like competing in a sporting event, giving an oral presentation, or talking to a boy you like.
- Someone said something mean to you and you can't get it out of your mind, so you think about it nonstop instead of drifting off into dreamland.

- The hormonal fluctuations of premenstrual syndrome, or PMS, may interfere with your sleep. Also, an adolescent brain is very different from the brain of a child. You process more, are aware of more, and this can keep you up at night.

Unlike self-imposed sleep deprivation, like when you stay up late to watch a movie or to finish homework, insomnia does not end with the promise of sweet dreams. In fact, it feels like there's no sleep in sight. You feel trapped, knowing that you'll have a hard time functioning in the morning. That's because insomnia can make you feel irritable, sluggish, foggy headed, anxious, depressed, and absolutely exhausted the next day. Insomnia can even weaken your immune system so that you get sick more often.

Fortunately, some tried-and-true, scientifically proven techniques can help you get to sleep. The following stories show how three girls have used some of these techniques to turn insomnia into a state of blissful rest. Maybe their solutions will work for you too!

Julia

"My mind just wouldn't turn off."

Julia is 15. She describes herself as "very average." She has an older brother and a younger sister and she thinks being a "middle child" makes her feel less special.

Julia was very nervous about her first-semester grades last year, her first year of high school. She was used to being near the top of her class in middle school, but her high school is much bigger and much more competitive. She couldn't get to sleep for the week before finals, no matter how hard she tried. This made her even *more* nervous that she would do poorly for lack of rest.

It was like the harder I tried, the worse it was. I kept thinking I'd flunk English. I thought about tests and quizzes that I messed up. I thought I should have gone in for extra help but I didn't. My English teacher said he was available after class but I never went. This is all I thought about at night and when I finally did sleep for an hour or so, I had bad dreams about being late for a test. I totally didn't know how to turn my brain off. I wanted to sleep but I couldn't.

These are the techniques that helped Julia.

Closing the Files

In biology, Julia's teacher said that the brain stores information in files like a computer. That got Julia to thinking about how her brain stays on at night, like her computer does if she leaves the files open. She thought of a way to close down her thoughts, or "brain-files," so her brain could turn off and go to sleep.

I made up a routine to close down the files in my head. First I think about the things I did or the things that happened during the day that I didn't like and didn't want to repeat. I put that in a file. Then I think about the things that I liked about my day and the things that I wanted to happen again. I put that in a file. When I get a nervous feeling, I put that in a file. Then I imagine my brain-files closed out for the night. I think about my brain-computer asking me if I want to shut down and I imagine clicking "OK."

If I wake up and think of something I have to do the next day, I write it down—I keep a pencil and paper by my bed. Then I put the thought in an actual paper file in the morning, or sometimes I just throw it out because even though it felt important during the night, it's really irrelevant. Also, if I wake up, I don't look at the clock because if I do, I just get frustrated and it's harder to get back to sleep.

I was able to relax and get to sleep faster after a few nights of doing my closing-the-files routine. It really does help.

Night Yoga

Julia's mom is into yoga and showed her some poses that are good for insomnia. Now, if Julia can't get to sleep after closing her brain-files, she gets up and does a yoga pose for just a few minutes.

I used to laugh at my mom but now yoga helps me too. I feel very relaxed afterward and I usually get right to sleep. It even helps PMS, which definitely makes my insomnia worse. It's kind of amazing. Even if I don't feel like getting up, I'm always glad I did.

Julia's Yoga Poses

- **Forward bend.** First Julia stands a few inches from her bed, facing the bed. She bends down from her waist until her forehead rests on the edge of her bed. Julia then extends her arms out on the bed, palms down. She rests there for a minute or so, about 20 to 30 breaths. Then Julia takes her forehead and arms off her bed, steps back a little bit, and bends as far as she comfortably can from her waist. Then she clasps her elbows with her hands, resting the top of her head on her forearms. She hangs in this position for another minute. "My mom taught it to me. She says forward bends calm the mind."

- **Feet up the wall.** Julia lies down on her back, facing a wall, and swings her legs up so her feet are resting on the wall. Her butt is a few inches from the wall. Then she closes her eyes and puts her arms out to her sides and just breathes for a few minutes. NOTE: DO NOT DO THIS POSE if you are menstruating, although it can help you feel less tense before or after your period. "This pose completely relaxes me. If I do this for 5 or 10 minutes, I usually fall right to sleep afterward. I don't use a timer—I just listen to a couple slow, quiet songs."

● **Child's pose.** (It's most comfortable to do this pose on a carpet. If you don't have carpeted floors, use a towel, blanket, or yoga mat.) First, Julia kneels with her knees about 6 inches apart, big toes lightly touching. Then she bends forward. She rests her chest on her thighs and rests her forehead on the floor. Julia places her hands on the floor next to her feet with palms facing up. (You can rest your forehead on a small pillow or folded towel.) Julia takes slow, deep breaths in this pose for a few minutes. "My mom says this is how a baby naturally rests in her crib. This is a very relaxing and calming pose."

Between her closing-the-files and night-yoga routines, Julia feels like she has some good ways to relax her mind and body.

This stuff has really helped me and now when I can't get to sleep I know what to do to help myself.

Alice

"My mind kept racing but my body wanted sleep so badly."

Alice is 16. She's an only child. Her parents got divorced when she was five and she spends most of her time with her mom. Her dad lives about a mile away from her mom, and Alice sees him on holidays and some weekends. Her dad remarried a few years ago and his new wife is nice to Alice and her mom.

Alice first started having sleep problems freshman year, when she developed anti-sleep habits that kept her awake during the day *and* night. Caffeine was the main culprit.

I started my day with a latte from the coffee shop. Then I had a diet cola at lunch and another one when I got home from school. I basically drank diet cola all night when I studied. And then I was wired when I wanted to go to bed. My heart raced and my feet twitched. My body was exhausted and in a way I felt overtired, like a cranky baby. I just couldn't sleep.

Alice tried some herbal remedies that are supposed to help insomnia, but they gave her heart palpitations. Here are some pro-sleep habits that really do work for her.

No Coffee or Caffeinated Cola After 2 P.M.

Research shows that if you have caffeine in your system after 2 P.M., it can keep you up at night. In fact, if you're sensitive to caffeine, a cup of coffee can affect you for up to 12 hours after you drink it. Alice still has her caffe latte in the morning and diet cola at lunch, but switched to caffeine-free cola when she gets home from school.

At first I thought it tasted different, but I got used to it. And it makes such a difference. It was totally worth the change. Sometimes I still miss the caffeine buzz I used to get to help me stay up to do homework, so I have a cup of hot chocolate after school. There's a little caffeine in it, but it doesn't bother me like regular diet cola did.

The Earplug Solution

Alice and her mom live in a small house and their bedrooms are right next to each other. Her mom usually stays up late watching television in her room, and the noise travels right into Alice's room too—she can hear everything. Alice realized that this was part of her sleeping problem. Then she found some foam earplugs at the drugstore that help dull the noise so she can get to sleep.

I bought these cheap little earplugs. They're just little foam things that you put in your ears and it blocks out the sound of the T.V. My boyfriend's sister told me that she uses earplugs in her dorm in college, and I thought it sounded like a good idea.

The CD Solution

Alice has another strategy for relaxing at night: She listens to a CD and keeps the volume turned down really low.

I take my portable CD player to bed, plug in the earphones, and listen to something relaxing. Right now I'm into jazz. The music is so soft I can barely hear it and it puts me to sleep like a lullaby—and it blocks out my mom's T.V.

My friend made me a mix of relaxing music for my birthday—they're all slow, mellow songs, all kinds of songs. She even put Louis Armstrong's "What a Wonderful World" on it. It's my favorite CD.

Wind-Down Time

Experts say that a moderate amount of exercise will help you get to sleep, but not right before you go to bed. It's important to give your mind and as well as your body 15 to 30 minutes of "wind-down time" at the end of your day.

Alice has always tried to be in bed by around 11 P.M., which is a pro-sleep habit—having a regular bedtime. But after her homework—mainly because she was so wired from all the caffeine—she'd do things that were *energizing*, like checking her E-mail and then doing 20 minutes on the treadmill. Instead of winding down for sleep, she was gearing up to stay awake.

I just changed my schedule. Now I get on the treadmill after school. It's actually better that way— it makes me more energetic when I need the energy. I check my E-mail after dinner, before homework. I also started taking bubble baths around 10:30. And after my bath, I read a little. I like poetry and right now I'm reading a collection of poems, A Night Without Armor, *by Jewel. I just read one or two poems in bed. They relax me.*

I like my new habits. And I'm sleeping much *better.*

Connie

"I would worry about my life instead of going to sleep."

Connie is almost 17 and a junior in high school. She's going to college in a year and a half and worries about her grades and ACT/SAT scores. Connie has two older sisters who go to her state's large university, but she's interested in a private liberal arts college. Connie's parents don't have a lot of money and they told her that if she wants to go to a private college, she has to get a big scholarship. Her grades matter a lot this year and she feels a lot of pressure.

Connie started having insomnia a few months ago after she had a nightmare.

I woke up, terrified, in the middle of the night. I dreamed I was living on the street, with no family and no job. First I thought I had a bad dream because I ate some chili right before I went to bed, but now I think I had the nightmare because I'm so anxious about my future. After that night, it's always been hard to get to sleep. I never had the nightmare again, but I do worry constantly about college and it keeps me up.

These things help Connie get to sleep.

Designated "Worry Time"

Connie realized that the problem was not that she worried about college—it was that she worried at the *wrong time* in her day. So she planned a "worry time" in which she allows herself to obsess about test scores, grades, college choices, and so on. Now if she finds herself worrying when she's lying in bed, she writes down her concerns, and reminds herself that she'll worry about them tomorrow during her "worry time."

My worry time is the 15 minutes it takes to get to school, between 7:45 and 8 A.M. I take the bus and since most of my friends live close enough to walk to school, I usually sit by myself or next to someone I don't know. So I don't talk to anyone, I just sit there and worry if I want to. When the bus stops at school I try to stop my worrying. Sometimes that's hard but I try. This kind of helps me keep my worries in a special place. Then they don't keep me up at night so much.

Progressive Relaxation

Connie learned a system of progressive relaxation to release tension. This prepares her for sleep by getting her mind off her future—instead, she focuses on living in the present and "letting go."

Connie's Progressive Relaxation System. (Each time you breathe out, silently say to yourself "relax.") First, tense up your whole body—your feet, legs, torso, arms, hands, neck, jaw—take a deep breath and then relax everything as you breathe out (silently say to yourself "relax").

Then, starting with your feet again, tense them, take a deep breath and release them as you exhale (silently say to yourself "relax").

Next, tense your legs, take another deep breath, and relax them as you exhale (silently say to yourself "relax").

Next, tense up your torso—your tummy, buttocks, chest, and back—take a deep breath, exhale, and relax them (silently say to yourself "relax").

Then, tense up your fingers, arms, and shoulders—take a deep breath, exhale, and relax them (silently say to yourself "relax").

Then, tense up your neck and jaw—take a deep breath, exhale, and relax them (silently say to yourself "relax").

Finally, without tensing first, take a deep breath and imagine that you are relaxing your brain and letting it drift back into your skull as you exhale (silently say to yourself "relax").

I learned how to do this in gym class one day. Our teacher was being nice to us and let us do "relax-o-gym." She said part of being physically fit is to know how to relax. I owe a lot to her because what she taught us helps me get to sleep.

The Subtraction Game

Sometimes Connie uses a mental game to get to sleep. She starts at 1,000 and subtracts 3 again and again.

I keep thinking I'll get to zero one time but I never have. I don't think I've ever gotten down below the 700s. This game either works right away or doesn't work at all for me.

A Light Snack

Connie used to go to bed either really hungry or really full—an anti-sleep habit. She experimented and learned that for her, eating a light snack about 30 minutes before bedtime helps her sleep.

I either snacked all night to stay awake so I could finish my homework or went to bed starving. When I ate a lot before bed I got an upset stomach, and if I was hungry I'd feel really nervous and kind of nauseous in bed.

For me, a banana and a glass of milk really help. I don't eat right before bed. I try to have my snack about 30 minutes to an hour before I go to bed. My friend likes graham crackers and milk for her bedtime snack, but I like my banana and milk snack better.

Visualization

Connie finds that visualizing a beautiful scene, like a quiet place on the beach, helps her feel content and relaxed—which keeps her mind away from the worries that interfere with a good night's sleep.

We live by Lake Michigan and I go to the beach a lot in the summer. I think about how beautiful the lake looks, with the sun shining and gulls flying around and the whitecaps that look to me like ponies galloping over the water. I think about how pretty it is on the beach and how peaceful I feel just looking at the lake. I think about this image a lot before I go to sleep. It works for me.

Summing It Up

Among the three of them, Julia, Alice, and Connie have a total of *11* pro-sleep habits. Hopefully, you can make at least one of these tools for sleep *your own*. See which ones work for you.

Are you logical and mathematical? Try Connie's Subtraction Game or Julia's Closing-the-Files strategy. Are you musical and meditative? Try Alice's CD solution. Or try Connie's Visualization. (Or just make up *your own* visualization!)

Tense when you pull down your covers? Try the progressive relaxation routine or night yoga. For more info on yoga and relaxation, visit *Yoga Journal's* website, yogajournal.com.

Do you thrive on caffeine? Try to stop imbibing after 2 P.M.—and see if you sleep better at night like Alice.

Some people only need just a few hours, some people need at least 10 hours—but most people need around 8 hours of sleep. And whether you need a little or a lot, the experts say that it's important to develop a consistent routine at bedtime. So experiment! Find one and stick with it. You'll feel so much more *fortified and balanced*, mentally and physically, with a full night's rest!

As Connie says, "I didn't used to know how to relax and go to sleep. Now I feel like I have some tools to do it."

Enough Already!

Bullies and So-Called Friends

No one likes to be teased about how they look. No one likes to be taunted because of her race or religion. No one likes to be pushed in the halls. No one likes to be laughed at and told she's a "reject." No one likes to eat lunch alone. No one likes to hear mean-spirited rumors that are flat out lies.

In other words, no one likes to be harassed by bullies. Yet surveys show that 86 percent of teens feel that harassment and bullying are *very common* at their schools—and studies show that almost one-third of kids have had a personal experience with bullies. So if you've ever been bothered by a bully, you're not alone.

All kids experiment with social power. It doesn't matter where you live or how big or small your school is—you will always run into cliques, clubs, and ring-leaders. School bullies are often the "popular kids"—if they don't like a girl, they can ridicule her and make her think she'll never have any friends. But, according to Dr. Michael Thompson, author of *Best Friends, Worst Enemies*, most kids who are excluded and bullied eventually find good friends.

Bullies may look like they're cool and confident, but inside they don't feel so great about themselves. That's one of the reasons they bully—to feel strong and powerful when inside they actually feel weak and insecure. In fact, it's not uncommon for kids within the "popular" group to dislike each other. They may keep up the appearance of friendships so that they won't be bullied or excluded *themselves*.

Studies tell us that girls bully just as much as boys, but girl bullies are different from boy bullies. Boys tend to bully in a physically aggressive way: pushing, shoving, tripping, and so on. Boys may also bully girls with rude sexual comments. On the other hand, girl bullies can be just as hurtful—on a *psychological and emotional* level. In other words, girl bullies are more likely to prey on the insecurities, fears, and weaknesses of their victims. As Rachel Simmons says in her bestseller, *Odd Girl Out*, girls' aggression is often "non-physical, indirect, and covert."

Girls tend to bully other girls in the following ways:

- Excluding a girl from birthday parties, lunch tables, and other social groups
- Spreading cruel rumors about a girl
- Making fun of a girl's appearance, race, religion, or family
- Making fun of a girl's intelligence
- Embarrassing a girl in public
- Pointing to a girl, then whispering and giggling
- Getting mad at a girl for no good reason, then "dropping" her from a group

Even friends can be bullies. If you can answer "yes" to any of the following questions, you may be a victim of "friend-bullying."

1. Does your friend make all the decisions in your relationship?
2. Is your friend constantly reminding you of or pointing out your bad points and problems?
3. Is your friend "two-faced" (being nice to you one minute, the next minute gossiping about you with others)?
4. Does your friend criticize your personality— does she tell you you're too shy or too loud? Too serious or too silly? Too dumb or too smart?
5. Does your friend try to talk you into doing things you know are wrong for you, like

    shoplifting, drinking, smoking, or drugs?
    Does she make fun of you if you say "no"?

6. Does your friend embarrass you in public?
7. Does your friend make plans with you, then cancels them if someone else asks her to do something?

Bullies are playing a power game. They try to control you by pretending they're more powerful than you—and when you cave in to them by acting powerless, they succeed. Bullies will eventually stop picking on you if you stop reacting like a victim. You'll spoil their fun if you ignore their insults. You'll be boring to them if you shoot them an "I have my own friends and I couldn't care less about you" or "I'm not intimidated by you" attitude.

Easier said than done? Sure. But don't think of it as impossible. Think of it as an opportunity to learn some REALLY IMPORTANT THINGS that every girl needs to know:

1. How to stick up for yourself
2. Who is a true, loyal friend and who is not
3. What you will do and what you won't do to keep a friend

Here are the stories of how three girls cope with bullies. It's hard, but they've all found ways to stop the bully-victim cycle. If you've been bullied, witnessed other people being bullied, or have bullied other people yourself, read on!

Anna

*"My best friend was more like
my worst enemy."*

Anna is 15 and a sophomore at a small public high school. She has two older brothers who are in college and one younger sister. Anna isn't particularly studious, but she does well in the classes she likes— English and art. Her mom works at an insurance company and her dad is a construction worker. She gets along pretty well with her family.

Anna has always had a close best friend. But last year, she realized that her "best friend" really wasn't a friend at all. She used to embarrass Anna in front of people every day at school.

We were best friends in eighth grade. She was beautiful, thin, popular, and a straight-A student. She was amazing at tennis. I used to look up to her and was completely intimidated by her. I thought she was cool and I did everything she wanted me to do. She'd be nice to me when we hung out together in private—but in front of other people, she was a total bitch.

Then the first day of freshman year, Anna's "best friend" did something unthinkable. She screamed at Anna at the top of her lungs in the halls at school, calling her names like "ho" and "stupid ass."

Everyone could hear her. I felt like crawling into a hole. And she did it every day for months—I think it was around six months. She made me feel soooo bad about myself because all I wanted to do was please her. I would come home from school and call her and cry on the phone. She told me I was taking things too seriously, like I was too sensitive. She said she'd stop screaming at me, but then she'd do it all over again.

Finally, Anna began to question the friendship. She decided that real friends don't scream at or embarrass each other. Anna decided that the only way to deal with her humiliation was to fight back. Here's how she did it.

A Dose of Her Own Medicine

(Note: This is a gutsy solution and it may not work for everyone. In fact, there's a chance it may backfire on you—but if you're sure that you're in a safe situation, it can be really effective.) Anna decided to give her "best friend" a dose of her own medicine—in other words, she decided to *scream back* at her. Anna's first step was to practice screaming back in front of her bedroom mirror. That helped her get the courage to scream back at her "best friend" in person, when the time felt right.

I practiced for a few days and then one day something inside me just snapped. She started screaming at me in the halls, in front of a whole group of kids, and I just let her have it. I just couldn't be passive with her anymore.

I screamed back at her, "Who do you think you are, acting superior and putting other people down? What right do you have to make other people feel bad about themselves? You think you're special, but you're just mean to people." Then I asked her, "Do you have anything else to say?" She just looked at me dumbfounded. So I said, "I didn't think so" and I walked away. Everyone cheered me!

Ever since that day, she never screamed at me again. And I'm not so afraid of people who try to intimidate me anymore.

Expanding the Options

Starting in third grade, Anna had always had a one-on-one, "best friend" friendship style. But now that she's older, she realizes that this system has a major flaw: She never had a plan B if the relationship had problems. Also, if the best friend wasn't available for some reason, she had no one to hang out with.

Anna made a goal for herself: To expand her friendship options so that she'd have more than just one friend.

I started talking to some girls I met in my gym class. They were really nice and now we sit together every day at lunch and we talk to each other after school. There are four of us and we're all nice to each other.

I also joined the art club and met some nice kids there. Two of the girls from my gym class are also in art club, so we have something in common to talk about.

I'm not that close to those girls, but I think it's OK. Maybe I'll feel closer to them later. In a way having only one friend is too intense. I'm having more fun and I'm happier now.

Laurie

"They wouldn't stop teasing me. The worse I felt, the more they laughed."

Laurie is 13 and goes to a big middle school in a big city. Her parents are both elementary school teachers. Laurie's the oldest of three girls, and her two younger sisters are tall and athletic. But Laurie's a bad athlete; she's short and undeveloped compared to the other girls in her class and wears glasses with thick lenses. Earlier in the year—at the beginning of eighth grade—two girls from the "popular" gang tried to intimidate her, making her life miserable for months.

They teased me about my appearance and they were really cruel. They called me "geeky" and "dorky." They pointed at me and whispered and laughed at me in class. They ran in back of me in the halls and stepped on my heels. It was just awful. I used to cry every day when I got home from school.

Sometimes I'd even pretend I was sick so I didn't have to go to school and deal with them.

Laurie tried telling the mean girls to stop but it didn't work.

I asked them why they were mean to me when they didn't even know me. They just laughed. I think they felt good that they were upsetting me, like they had won or something. It got even worse after that. In retrospect, I think it's better not to show them that you're upset or affected in any way.

Laurie talked to her mom, and they came up with **Laurie's Anti-Bully Strategies** that did work.

The Non-Reaction Reaction

When the bullies start to tease her, Laurie pretends they're talking in a language she doesn't understand, like they're from a different planet. She shows absolutely no sign that she is aware that the girls are even talking to her, or talking about her. She doesn't give them the pleasure of feeling like they've "gotten to her." Laura just looks right past them and walks away.

I learned from experience that reacting to them is just what they want, so I play this game with them and pretend I have no idea what they're saying and no interest in their language.

I honestly pretend that they're from some faraway planet like Pluto. I say to myself, "They're talking Plutonian and you don't understand Plutonian." I don't even look at them. So they don't get the reaction they want from me. At first they tried harder and harder to get my attention, but after a week or so they got bored and stopped being so stupid.

The Buddy System

The times Laurie was bullied most often were the times she was alone in the halls or walking home alone from school. So now, Laurie makes it a point to walk with her friends between classes, go to the bathroom with friends, eat lunch with friends in the cafeteria, and walk home with friends or her sisters. The fact that Laurie is constantly surrounded by her own friends is a bully-deterrent.

I talked this strategy over with a couple of my friends, and we all agreed to look out for each other. I found out that another one of my friends gets teased too. Most of my friends are in my classes, and I got my locker changed so now I'm next to a good friend. So it's pretty easy not to be alone in the halls. Being with a friend makes me feel much more comfortable at school now.

Telling a Teacher

Laurie initially didn't want to tell a teacher that the girls were mean to her, but her mom encouraged her to do it as a last resort. So far, she's only had to do this once.

The hardest time is recess, because everyone's running all over the place when it's nice out and we go outside. One time the mean girls were throwing stones at me and my friends. We told the teacher who was on the playground, and she made them stop.

I used to care what those mean girls thought about me but now I don't. If they want to think I'm a baby because I told on them, that's their problem. I think it's more important to take care of me than to care about what they think about me. And guess what! They leave me alone now!

Lucinda

"I didn't think I was really hurting anyone. It was like a game."

Lucinda is 15. She grew up being teased 24/7 by her four older brothers. They teased her about *everything*: her weight, her good grades—even her hair, which is really curly. Lucinda's parents both work full-time and aren't around after school, which is when the teasing was the worst.

It was a vicious cycle. Lucinda would tell her mom about her brothers, and they'd get punished. But then they'd call her a "goody-goody" and tease her even more when her parents weren't home. In short, Lucinda felt like a big loser because of the constant teasing.

Now three of her brothers don't live at home anymore, and she gets along OK with the brother who's still in high school. Still, she feels that being teased at home made her act like a bully at school a few years ago.

When I got teased all the time, it sure felt good to tease somebody else. I feel terrible about it now, but it really made me feel more powerful, like I was OK after all. I sure didn't feel OK at home. I felt like a big, ugly creep, which is what my oldest brother used to call me.

The object of Lucinda's teasing was a girl who was the shortest person in her gym class. No one wanted this girl on her team and Lucinda teased and taunted her about this nonstop.

I called her "klutzy" and "shrimp" and "loser." I did it for attention. When I called her names the other kids laughed and I felt cool.

Then the girl left school and went to a private school. Lucinda found out by the grapevine that *she* was responsible for the girl transferring schools.

The older sister of one of my friends went out with this girl's brother, and he said I was the reason. I

*teased her so much she had to leave school. It made
me feel really bad. I was just having fun. I just
wanted to be cool like my brothers. I never realized I
was hurting her that bad.*

Shortly after the girl transferred schools, Lucinda's
mom found her crying in her room. Lucinda told her
mom everything. And her mom had a story to share.

When her mom was Lucinda's age, there was a
sickly girl in her class. The teachers told the kids to
be nice to this girl because she was sick, but no one
listened. They teased her because she couldn't ever
take gym and had to take lots of pills at lunch. Once
someone put a dead spider on her desk and she
screamed. Kids made her cry all the time with their
teasing. Then one day, the teacher said she died.

*My mom said she felt so bad. She kept asking
herself, "Why didn't I get it? Why didn't I stop the
teasing? Why did I have no empathy for her?" This
happened 30 years ago, and my mom still feels bad.
I never wanted to feel guilt like that. I feel bad for my
mom but it made me decide that I'll never bully
anyone, ever again. She said that's why she shared
the story with me—so I'd understand how serious
bullying can be.*

Turning a Negative into a Positive
Like so many difficult situations, Lucinda's experience
as a bully was a lesson that changed her life for the
better. After she was able to *observe* herself, she

wanted to *change* herself—and she was able to turn her bullying behavior into *compassionate* behavior.

Lucinda decided to turn a bad experience into a good one. Her solution: Stop being a bully and start being an *advocate* for kids who are bullied.

I was really able to look at myself and say to myself that I didn't want to bully anyone. I realized I was just doing to others like my brothers were doing to me. But it was worse, because I picked on a weak person who couldn't fight back. Instead of fighting back, she just changed schools.

Now, when I see a kid being picked on, I automatically stick up for him or her. Instead of making kids feel bad, I want to make them feel good. Now I feel like it's my job to help the underdog. I get my friends to stick up for the weak kids too.

I honestly think some bullies have no idea how much they're hurting a kid by picking on her. That was the case with me. I thought it was all funny. I didn't think about her feelings, only my own. So now I'll say to someone, "How would you like it if someone harassed you the way you harass everyone?" On one occasion I helped a girl see that she was causing misery on someone else, and she stopped the bully garbage.

I know I'm not a bad person; I just made some mistakes. But I'm also helping to stop bullying in my school, and I feel good about that. I even participated in a presentation to the school board about how to deal with bullying in high school.

Without my experience as a bully, I could never have done that. I would never have been interested.

Summing It Up

Anna, Laurie, and Lucinda were *all* victims of bullying. But their experiences were quite different and so were their responses.

Anna was bullied by a so-called "best friend." Laurie was bullied by mean, insecure girls—the "popular" gang of girls at school. Initially Anna and Laurie caved in to the bullies—they didn't stick up for themselves, which made them even more tempting targets.

Lucinda was bullied by her brothers. Ultimately, Lucinda dealt with her bad feelings by picking on a weak girl and being a bully herself.

All three girls had very different strategies for coping with bullies. Think about what might work best for you.

- You may decide to scream back at them, like Anna. (But first make sure you're safe and have friends around you.)
- You may pretend they're speaking Plutonian and walk away, like Laurie.
- Maybe you'll decide to widen your circle of friends, or surround yourself at all times with the friends you have now.
- You could join a student group to learn some skills to help you cope with bullies and aggression.

- You could join a student group that works against bullies. (Ask your school social worker or advisor if these kinds of groups exist at your school. If not, ask if you could start one!)
- You could help someone who's being bullied, like Lucinda, instead of being an "innocent bystander" or even a bully yourself.

Get some ideas from Anna, Laurie, and Lucinda. If you're still having a hard time thinking of strategies, you could ask for help from your parents, a friend, a teacher, or another trusted adult.

Experts agree that being bullied in middle school and high school *does not* lead to a girl never having friends. It's more likely to be a hard period of time, which is *temporary*.

The important thing is to make friends with kids who share your values, who you genuinely like, and who are nice to you. By the time you're finished with high school, chances are that you'll learn that some friends are loyal and others will betray you. And you'll learn the value of a *true* friendship, where you are liked for who you are, period.

As Anna says, "Now I look for people I can be myself with. You shouldn't have to bend yourself for people to like you. You shouldn't have to put up with being bullied because it's the bullies that have the problem, not you."

When Your Crush Is a Girl

Lesbian Teens

Asking yourself who you genuinely are is the grand riddle of your life. The answer is yours and yours alone. It's personal. It will affect how you see yourself, how you behave, and how you fit into the world. And your sexual identity is just a piece of the puzzle.

Do you wonder what it would be like to kiss a girl? When you hook up with a guy, do you get bored and fantasize about the softness of a woman? Do you like guys, but prefer to spend time with your female friends? Are you curious about lesbians?

Are you scared these feelings are abnormal?

Well, they're not. And having these feelings doesn't necessarily mean that you're gay. It's not unusual for two girls to hug and hold hands and be

195

close. It's not unusual for girls to look forward to being together after school and on weekends. It's also very common for a girl's first sex-play experience to be with another girl.

But perhaps you're interested in exploring the possibility that you are romantically attracted to girls, or that you're attracted to girls as well as boys.

Maybe you're just going through a phase. Or maybe you are a lesbian or bisexual. According to Dr. Barbara Kelly—a therapist in the Chicago area who specializes in working with lesbian, gay, bisexual, and transsexual clients—some girls don't make this decision until they're almost 20 or even older. Still, it's natural to start wondering about your sexual identity in your preteens.

As a matter of fact, you may be wondering about a lot of things about yourself: Do I have a good sense of humor, or do I just say funny things because I think my friends want to be entertained? Am I really a nice person, or do I do nice things so that people will like me? I hate shopping at discount stores—does this make me selfish and stuck-up? Am I really smart, or do I just make lucky guesses on tests?

You have lots of time to think about who you are and to explore your feelings. You have lots of time to experiment with different kinds of relationships. It's natural to be curious about different sexual lifestyles. If you think you might be a lesbian, support is out there for you.

So explore your feelings. Explore them with others; explore them in private. Respect the fact that you're an explorer. You're not abnormal. You're not weird. You may be gay, or you may not be gay. Some researchers think that as much as 10 percent of the population is gay, so if you are, you have lots of company. If your class has 500 kids in it, there are at least 50—and probably more—who are questioning themselves, just like you.

Do you have a friend who has told you she's gay? Does she scare you because you think she might have a crush on you and you're straight? Don't be afraid of her. She's most likely not attracted to you that way and not trying to have a sexual relationship with you. Try to understand her. Try to support her as a person. She feels the exact same kind of giddy, crazy excitement you feel when you see your crush—except that her crushes are girls and women. Try to understand that "different" doesn't mean "bad."

Here are the stories of three girls who think they are, or might be, lesbian or bisexual. They are courageous. They are independent and unique. They are resilient. Let them inspire you.

Lenni

"I really and truly think I'm special because I'm a lesbian."

Lenni is 17 and is president of her school's dance club. She comes from a family of eight and everyone still lives at home, so life can get pretty crowded and privacy is a valuable commodity. Lenni is close with her older sister (they share a room) and gets along OK with the rest of her brothers and sisters, all of whom are younger. Her parents both teach math at a parochial school, but Lenni and her brothers and sisters go to a big public high school located in their neighborhood.

Lenni first thought she might be a lesbian in sixth grade. From the beginning, she felt like she was special.

I didn't care what people thought. I was comfortable with myself. I've always liked makeup and getting all dressed up and doing my nails and stuff— and that doesn't mean anything. I mean, you can like girls and still be girly yourself.

I first thought I was a lesbian because I had the biggest crush on my gym teacher when I was 11. I dreamed about kissing her and touching her. Then I actually had a sexual experience with one of the girls on my basketball team in eighth grade. One day in the locker room she told me I was beautiful and that she was attracted to me. I felt the same about her and we dated in secret. Ever since then, I knew I liked girls. I never was attracted to boys at all. I think being a lesbian makes me different and unique and I like that.

Most of the people in Lenni's family know that she is a lesbian, but they don't really understand.

When I told my mom, she started crying. I felt so bad. I still feel bad about my mom. I never wanted to hurt her. As long as I don't talk about my girlfriends, she's fine. But sometimes when I go out she asks me who I'm going out with. If I tell her I'm going out with my girlfriend, she starts crying. I'm very sad about my mom.

My older sister was OK and my dad told me it was something from the devil! Can you believe that? I go to church every Sunday, and he thinks I'm like the devil!

In retrospect, I think I should have waited until I'm out of the house to come out to my family. I know my parents love me, but I know they're upset about it and I feel bad about that. I wish they could understand but I don't know if they ever will.

I have found some friends who are supportive of me, and that really helps my self-esteem, because in my opinion, I'm AWESOME!

Here's how Lenni keeps her self-esteem in the awesome range.

A Quest for Like-Minded People

Lenni found a group of people who are like her. This took a little perseverance, but her time and motivation paid off. After lots of phone calls, many of which led to dead ends, Lenni found a center that caters to gay and bisexual teens. She finds great comfort and support in the company of people who have experiences, thoughts, and feelings that she can relate to.

I found a place in the phone book and I called and they were real nice to me and told me about their teen group. That's where I met a lot of friends.

We have a saying in our group: "No one, but no one, can make it alone." It's a quote from Maya Angelou, and we made it our group slogan.

It helps to know other people like me. I can't stress that enough. We all tell each other, "Be who you are and don't care about what anyone else thinks."

Books

Someday Lenni wants to write a story about a non-stereotypical lesbian girl—so far it's been hard to find anything besides "Are you gay? This is how you know" kinds of books. But she has found a few books that she likes.

Reading stories about gay people makes me feel more normal. I can relate to them. I hate the books geared toward older people—like testimonies of gay men and women, or how hard life is for a queer teen. They're boring and preachy and it's not what I want to read.

I've found some good books. One is called Rubyfruit Jungle *and it's cool. You can probably find good books in the gay/lesbian section of a bookstore. You can order them online if you don't want to buy them at a bookstore. I get lots of used books online, and I get some real bargains.*

A Creative Project

Lenni's taking a photography class in school and loves it. She also loves to make collages. So she put these two passions together and made a huge collage of women. It hangs in her room—and just looking at it makes Lenni feel proud.

I took some pictures of women—my mom and grandmom and sisters and friends and mostly strangers—women sitting on benches in the park, women strolling babies, women on the beach, women with big hats, and women of all shapes, sizes, and ages. Then I cut pictures out of magazines—sexy models mostly—and made a collage out of my photographs and the magazine pictures.

I used a huge piece of blue poster board for the background. Then I cut out the words "Girls Rule" and "Girl Power" and things like that from magazines, and glued them around the edges of my collage. It's really cool. The collage represents all different kinds of women, and reminds me how cool women are, and how cool I am.

I think doing something creative, no matter what it is, helps you express yourself. At least it does for me.

Brenna

"I have been confused for so long. I think I'm straight but I have crushes on girls too. Maybe I'm bisexual. I don't know."

Brenna is 16 and lives with her mother and stepfather, plus two siblings—an older sister and a younger brother. She has a good relationship with her mom, but no relationship with her stepfather. Brenna's "real" father left when she was four and now lives in South America. Brenna has been playing soccer since she could walk and is on her school's varsity team.

Brenna was 13 when she started to wonder: "Am I straight or 'bi'?" She is still bewildered by this question.

In seventh grade, I thought I couldn't be like that [bisexual]. I didn't want to be. I thought I had to change and I felt weird 'cause I really liked a girl on my soccer team a lot but at the same time I didn't want to admit my feelings.

Then I talked to my sister and she said, "No, you're not like that. You're being weird. You're just confused. Don't even think about it anymore." She said I was hanging out with bad kids, and she'd never ever talk to me again if I was gay. But I couldn't not think about it. I didn't know what to do.

Lots of boys ask Brenna out, and this has added to her confusion.

I have many chances to go out with boys and I do go out with them. I like them. But I have strong feelings for girls too. I have crushes on girls and guys.

I feel very mixed up because I don't know what I want sometimes and I am afraid I might want the other sex, like if I have a boyfriend I wish I could be with a girl. I'm still in the process of working this out but right now I think I'm attracted to boys more than girls.

Here's what helps Brenna cope with her many different feelings about exploring her sexuality.

Talking to Trusted Friends

Brenna knew some girls at school who were lesbians and she decided to talk with them. She was afraid her straight friends wouldn't understand how confused she felt—after all, her own sister couldn't even offer her support.

I don't want a lot of people to know. There's a group at my school for gays, but I'd never go. Everyone would find out. My school is very anti-gay. People spit at gay kids and call them the worst names. Some schools aren't like this. I read in the paper about a school that voted two girls as the "cutest couple" of the senior class. I think all schools should be like that.

I decided to tell two girls I know who are gay. I just told them that I think I might like girls but I'm not sure. I'm glad they came out to me a while ago, because that made it easier for me to talk to them. Girls should do that—come out so other girls can come out.

Brenna's gay friends gave her the support she needed; as she talked with them, she felt more comfortable about questioning her sexuality.

I told them that I like dating guys, but I think I might like girls too. I was so confused. My friends were cool. They said that if I can imagine having a romantic and sexual relationship with a guy, that I'm probably not a lesbian—that I'm straight or maybe I'm bi. They said if I keep feeling attracted to girls, I should try being with them. If I don't like it, I'm straight and if I do, I'm bi.

Brenna isn't ready to make a decision about her sexuality right now. She's decided to keep her mind open, read some books, and continue to date boys.

I'm not ready to try being with a girl now, but if I want to do that I will someday. My friends understand my feelings and they tell me that I'm their friend no matter what way I am. That has made all the difference to me. The fact that they accept me for who I am makes me calm down and feel like I'm not a complete weirdo.

Thinking Ahead to a Self-Fulfilling Future

Brenna feels that her self-esteem is in pretty good shape. She thinks that one of the main reasons that she feels OK about herself is that she has goals for her future. And her future is bright! She works hard in school, plans to go to college, and wants to be a psychologist or an architect when she's older.

The last thing I want to be is like my mom. No offense to her, she's a great mom, but I do not want to stay home and cook and clean like her. I want a career and I want to make some money of my own.

So I think about that, and I feel good about myself and love myself. I know deep in my heart that no matter if I'm straight or bi, I'll do good things with my life.

Helene

"I always knew I liked girls."

Helene is 18 and has been working as a workshop facilitator for lesbian and bisexual teens since she graduated high school last year. She lives in the Chicago area with her mom and younger sister. She fights with her mom sometimes about when she can spend time with her girlfriend—but in general, Helene gets along pretty well with her family. At this point in her life, Helene feels good about the fact that she is who she is, including the fact that she is gay—but this was not always the case. For years, she was insecure about herself and pretended to be someone she's not.

Even at a young age, Helene always knew she was attracted to females.

My first best friend and I used to kiss each other on the lips all the time when we were in kindergarten or first grade. That doesn't necessarily mean you're gay but I knew I was, even then. I just felt different somehow. I was a tomboy too. I hated dolls and stuff, although I know some women who hated dolls when they were little but now they're happy with men. My friend moved when we were eight, but I often wonder if she's a lesbian too—the last I heard, she had a baby boy, but who knows? She could be attracted to girls or in the closet.

When she was 17, just after she graduated high school, Helene told her mom she was gay. This was hard, but by that time Helene had become more secure about herself. She also became involved with her current girlfriend and was tired of living a lie at home. Plus, Helene felt she was finally at the point where she thought she could handle her mom's reactions, no matter what they were.

It was scary to come out to my mom but I had to tell her and my grandmom and my sister because after a while, everyone else knew and I didn't want it to get to them through word of mouth. Finally, I was mature enough and comfortable enough to tell them that Rosalind was much more than my best friend. I had to tell them for my own self-respect.

Actually my grandmom is supportive. She likes my girlfriend. My mom and sister are OK but sometimes my sister says things to get under my skin, like if I had gone to a coed school, I wouldn't be so "confused." That pisses me off because I know who I am and I know what I like.

I get along with my mom OK but she gets in the way of my relationship a lot, as far as attempting to tell me when I can spend time with my girlfriend. But

I'm saving money to move into an apartment so she won't be able to interfere soon.

Now peoples' responses don't really matter to me, because I'm still going to do my thing. If they don't like me because I'm gay, they don't have to be around me because now I love how I am. And I have to live my life.

Here's what helped Helene accept her sexuality and love who she is.

Sharing the Secret
High school was hell for Helene.

I never dressed like a "typical girl." I never wore makeup and my hair was really short. All the kids made fun of me. They teased me and called me a "gay-ass bitch." It was horrible. I had to pretend I was someone I wasn't. I went out with boys but I wasn't interested in them except as friends. I can't say that it didn't cross my mind to jump out of a window.

Finally, when Helene was 15, she felt she had to tell someone that she didn't look like a "typical girl" because she *wasn't* a "typical girl."

I cried because I couldn't hold it in anymore, and so many people kept bringing up my style of dress and making comments about how I will never dress like a girl and how I carried myself like a tomboy and that I should be growing out of that stage. I felt bad and awkward, like I was some kind of freak or something. But I had too much pride to deny myself, to be someone I'm not, so I just came out to my best friend.

I just had to share my feelings with someone. This might not be the best thing for everyone, but for me it was the thing to do.

It happened sort of naturally. My best friend was teasing me about "really liking" our mutual friend who was 20 at the time, and I said, "Yeah, you got me." At first she was shocked. Then she was like "Are you serious? Don't bullshit me, all jokes aside." I told her yeah, I was serious and that I like girls. Then I named all the girls that I like and she was like "cool." That was the end of it. I think I must have felt comfortable telling her because I trusted that she would understand somehow.

In retrospect, I took a big risk. She could have laughed at me and told people. If you tell someone, you have to be sure that you can trust him or her. Then last year, on Mother's Day, she told me that she likes girls too—just like I told her, except that we were 17 and way more mature about the matter.

Gay Teen Support Group

With the exception of a couple of very close friends, Helene virtually denied her sexuality to everyone all through her freshman and sophomore years of high school. She felt insecure and didn't want to be labeled by people who were prejudiced against gays.

Then in her junior year, Helene found out about a group for gay teens that gave her the support she needed to feel good about herself.

I found out about a media activism program for gay teens. I heard about it from a friend of mine who was in a dance corps with me. Her sister was facilitating the group at the time. We wrote letters to magazines, organized protests, things like that. We supported each other for being who we are. The group helped me open up and be proud of myself. It was a turning point for me.

Now I facilitate a gay-teen workshop—it's my job. It feels good to help another. I was in their shoes once upon a time, so I love doing that job.

A Gay Mentor

It can feel good to have a "mentor"—an older, wiser person to whom you can bring questions and concerns. A person who won't judge you but will help guide you to be the best person you can be.

Helene found such a person in an older friend, Kay. When Helene was 15, Kay, then 21, came out to her. Ever since then, Helene has relied on Kay for advice from time to time.

We talk about girls and issues like how to treat a woman well. I have learned so much from her. I was something else when I was younger. It sounds weird, but I had no respect for women at all, but she would put me in place when I was out of line and guide me to respect women. I've changed drastically since then—I just needed to mature and learn from experience.

Now I'm in love and I treat my lady like the queen she is, but if I need a few pointers from Kay, from how to stop this problem or argument to how to give my lady a romantic evening, then I'll ask Kay every now and then. Now I'm usually the gay mom to my younger friends. I like helping other people find their own path because I know how much help I got, and get, from Kay.

Summing It Up

Helene, Brenna, and Lenni all found strength from SUPPORT SYSTEMS—people to talk to about their thoughts and feelings, even when their feelings are confusing and troubling.

Helene found her support system in several places. First, in her best friend, who was cool and accepting. Also, in a media action support group for gay teens at her school that gave Helene friendships and a positive outlet for her energy. Helene was also lucky enough to find a "gay mom" who, for years, has been a good friend and mentor.

Many schools have gay/straight alliance (GSA) clubs—clubs that are made up of all sorts of people, gay and straight. The purpose of a GSA club is to make the world a fair and safe place for everyone. You won't be judged for being different. And you can meet other kids who are questioning their sexuality. By definition, the members are open-minded people who accept—and value—diversity.

So find a group or club! Look for flyers, look in your school catalog, ask around. If you're too shy or embarrassed to ask someone in person, make an anonymous call to your school, or check the school's website for info. Or check your community for gay teen groups. With perseverance, you'll probably find a group where you feel you can fit in, like Lenni and Helene did.

Not sure whether you're gay or straight or somewhere in between? This was the case for Brenna. She didn't feel comfortable going to a group; she found her support system in some special friends. So don't give up! Find someone to talk to, even if that means going to a counselor for help and support.

Be creative! Celebrate your passion! Make a collage, like Lenni. Read books about resilient lesbian and bi teens. (For some good books, see Resources for Your Journey.) Think of your own power, and make goals for a bright future, like Brenna.

Feed your self-esteem with support and inspiration, and watch it grow.

Helene, Brenna, and Lenni are learning to love themselves for who they are. We can all learn from them. It doesn't matter if you're gay or straight: Try to love yourself and be proud of yourself for your individuality. Remember, being a lesbian or bisexual may not be the lifestyle of the majority of girls and women, but it's still a shade of normal. Even if you're not gay, this is a big, important concept that can help make the world a better place for everyone.

As Helene says, "If you are questioning then go ahead and give it a try. If *you* [not others] like it then stick with it, if not then don't. But always, always, always remember to do what makes you happy and follow what your heart tells you to do. Also, don't feel pressured to stick a label on yourself. Labels should stay on cans in a store—they are not needed for people."

Afterword

Landing on Your Feet

All the solutions, or ruby slippers, in this book are meant to help you start your own private collection. Try them on for size. Gather up the ones that fit and put them in your closet of *inner strength* and *capabilities*. The more crowded your inner closet, the better. You can never have too many ruby slippers, and best of all, like self-love and self-respect, they're absolutely free!

I like to think that ruby slippers come in unlimited shapes and sizes. When you've worn the same slippers for a while, it's fun to think of trying on a new pair. Will they bring you fresh solutions to old problems? Will you feel a deeper sense of inner power and peace? Or will you discard them in favor of a new—or old—pair? One thing I know is for sure: the more pairs of ruby slippers you have in your closet, the more likely you'll be to land safely outside the tornados of stress and despair that life sometimes brings.

Go shopping for more ruby slippers when you feel sad, confused, or stressed out. Sometimes they turn up in unexpected places, like in overheard conversations, in dreams, or while looking at a flower. Sometimes they're right in front of you, like in advice from your best friend or even your mom (don't you hate it when she's right?!). Don't be afraid to discard ruby slippers, wherever they come from, that DON'T work for you. Throw them out to make room for new ones that fit just right.

Wherever you find ruby slippers, wear them with pride. Have the inner knowledge that, like Dorothy, your power lies at your feet, just waiting to be tapped.

Resources for Your Journey

ere are some books, articles, videos, websites, and other tidbits that the girls you met recommend to *you*. You can find most of the books in a bookstore or library. Or try finding them online.

Body Image/Eating Healthy

Teri's Recommendations

Acts of Love (a novel) by Judith Michael, Crown
  Publishers, 1997. (Touching, romantic story about
  a woman who comes to terms with her body
  image and self-esteem issues—recommended for
  older teens.)

No Body's Perfect: Stories by Teens About Body Image, Self-Acceptance and the Search for Identity by Kimberly Kirberger, Scholastic, 2003. (Inspirational narratives by girls who have overcome body image problems and eating disorders—a really good book.)

Strong Women Stay Young by Miriam E. Nelson, Bantam Books, 1997. (Good info and instructions on strength training.)

A Teen's Guide To Going Vegetarian by Judy Krizmanic, Puffin Books, 1994.

Jenny's Recommendations

Body Traps by Judith Rodin, Quill William Morrow, 1992. (Good info on body image plus lots of interesting self tests.)

I'm Gonna Like Me: Letting off a Little Self-Esteem by Jamie Lee Curtis, HarperCollins, 2002. (A little kids' book, but really cool nevertheless. Read it to kids you baby-sit for or to your little sister or brother.)

Amy's Recommendations

Creative Visualization by Shakti Gawain, New World Library, 2002. (One of the very best books on affirmation and visualization, ever. Techniques are practical and easy to understand. This 25th anniversary edition is updated from the original.)

Teenage Fitness: Get Fit, Look Good, and Feel Great! by Kathy Kaehler, HarperCollins, 2001. (Good tips for a healthy—not obsessive—exercise plan.)

Other Stuff of Interest
"An Image To Heal" by Jill S. Zimmerman, *The Humanist*, Jan/Feb 1997. (This article discusses the media's effect on women's body image.)

Organizations and Websites
Anorexia Nervosa & Associated Disorders (ANAD)—For anorexics and bulimics
> Hot line: 847-831-3438.
> Website: anad.org.
> Call or log on for information. They will also help you find a therapist, physician, nutritionist, and/or self-help group in your area.

Overeaters Anonymous (OA) National Organization—For compulsive overeaters
> Info line: 505-891-2664
> Website: oa.org
> Call or log on for information. They will also help you find a self-help group in your area.

Panic Attacks/Anxiety

Rebecca's Recommendation
Master Your Panic and Take Back Your Life! by Denise Beckfield, Impact Publishers, Inc., 1998. (Good strategies for dealing with panic attacks.)

Mary's Recommendations
Illuminated Prayers by Marianne Williamson, Simon & Schuster, 1997. (Little book with pretty illustra-

tions and short prayers—can give you ideas for
your own prayers. Spiritual—not religious.)

Website: panicdisorder.about.com/cs/copingwith911
/index.htm (Good info about all kinds of anxiety
problems.)

Laura's Recommendations

The Complete Book of Essential Oils & Aromatherapy
   by Valerie Ann Worwood, New World Library,
   1991. (All you need to know about aromatherapy,
   including a list of oils and their effects on your
   well-being.)

Website: firehotquotes.com (Pages and pages of
quotes you can use in a quotation journal—some
funny, some serious. You can even submit your
own!)

Feeling Down

Kelly's Recommendations

*The Don't Sweat Affirmations: 100 Inspirations to
   Help Make Your Life Happier & More Relaxed* by
   editors of Don't Sweat Press (foreword by Richard
   Carlson), Hyperion, 2001. (Uplifting thoughts for
   when you feel down.)

Cheesy Movies: *Crossroads* with Britney Spears,
Legally Blonde with Reese Witherspoon

Tameeka's Recommendations
The Everything Soup Cookbook by J. J. Hanson, Adams
Media Corporation, 2002.

Website for incense: mothersbooks.org (For Amma's
Rose incense—Tameeka's favorite.)

Classical CDs: *The Beautiful Voice* by opera star
Renée Flemming, Decca, 1998. Any CD by Handel,
Mozart, Bach, or Beethoven.

Sami's Recommendations
Tearjerker movies: *On Golden Pond*, with Jane Fonda,
Henry Fonda, and Katharine Hepburn. (Bittersweet
story—with a sad ending—about how a woman tries
to reconnect with her father.) *Terms of Endearment*,
with Jack Nicholson, Shirley Maclaine, and Debra
Winger. (Complex mother-daughter relationship
with a sad twist.)

Other Stuff of Interest
Feeling Good: The New Mood Therapy by David
   Burns, Signet Books, 1980. (Offers new ways to
   look at your thoughts and explains how irrational
   thoughts can affect your feelings.)
*I Will Remember You: What to Do When Someone You
   Love Dies* by Laura Dower, Scholastic Inc., 2001.
The Right Words at The Right Time edited by Marlo
   Thomas, Atrai Books, 2002. (Inspiring personal
   essays about how words and ideas have changed
   lives for the better.)

*When Nothing Matters Anymore: A Survival Guide For
   Depressed Teens* by Bev Cobain (Kurt's cousin),
   Free Spirit Publishing, 1998.

Website: nostigma.com (Website of National Mental
Health Awareness Campaign—helpful info on biological and/or chronic depression for you or someone you love.)

Guys

Sarah's Recommendation
*The Go Ask Alice Book of Answers: A Guide to Good
   Physical, Sexual, and Emotional Health* by
   Columbia University's Health Ed. Program, Henry
   Holt & Co., 1998. (See "Relationship" section for
   some thoughtful answers to some difficult
   questions.)

Gracie's Recommendations
Planned Parenthood website: plannedparenthood
.org
Planned Parenthood hot line: 1-800-230-PLAN (Call
for info or to make an appointment at a center in
your area.)

Emma's Recommendation
*Changing Bodies, Changing Lives: A Book for Teens on
   Sex and Relationships*, 3rd edition by Ruth Bell,
   Random House, 1998. (See "Changing Sexuality"
   chapter for really good info on sex and sexuality.)

Smoking, Drinking, Drugs

Sue's Recommendation

1440 Reasons to Quit Smoking: One For Every Minute of the Day by Bill Didds, Meadowbrook Press, 2000. (Just like it says—tons of reasons that may help you in your weak moments.)

Meredy's Recommendation

Normal Girl: A Novel by Molly Jong-Fast, Villard Books, 2001. (Intense story about a girl who had it all—money, famous parents, a boyfriend, parties—and her road from addiction to recovery.)

Sarine's Recommendations

Go Ask Alice by Anonymous, ed. by Beatrice Sparks, Pocket Books, 1998. (Harrowing story, in diary form, about a girl who does drugs.)

The Other Great Depression: How I'm Overcoming on a Daily Basis at Least a Million Addictions and Finding a Spiritual (Sometimes) Life by Richard Lewis, Plume Books, 2000. (Inspiring—and at times hilarious—recovery story of the famous comedian.)

Overscheduled Life/Stress

Andie's Recommendation

100 Simple Secrets of Happy People: What Scientists Have Learned & How You Can Use It by David Niven, HarperCollins, 2000. (Ideas that can help you put your schedule—and your life—in perspective.)

Cara's Recommendations

The Absolute Beginner's Guide to Origami: The Simple Three-Stage Guide to Creating Expert Origami by Nick Robinson, Watson-Guptill Publications, 1999.

Knitting Basics: All You Need to Know to Take Up your Needles and Get Knitting by Betty Barnden, Barrons, 2002.

Meditation for Dummies: A Reference for the Rest of Us by Stephan Bodian, Hungry Minds, 1999. (The title may sound silly, but this is a really good book on meditation.)

Shelley's Recommendations

Shelley loved these real-life stories.

Seabiscuit: An American Legend by Laura Hillenbrand, Ballantine Books, 2001. (A great bio on the famous racehorse.)

Wise Girl: What I've Learned About Life, Love, and Loss by Jamie-Lynn Sigler, Pocket Books, 2002. (The popular actress shares her life story and the wisdom she's gained.)

Novels—These are all really good reads that will "take you away from it all":

Angus, Thongs and Full Frontal Snogging: Confessions of Georgia Nicolson by Louise Rennison, HarperCollins, 2001. (Funny story about the big events in a 14-year-old British girl's life.)

Animal Dreams by Barbara Kingsolver, Harper-
 Collins, 1991. (Great "coming of age" story—
 recommended for older teens.)

Hope Was Here by Joan Brauer, Putnam, 2000.
 (Warm, engaging story about a 16-year-old girl's
 life as a waitress.)

The Princess Diaries series by Meg Cabot, Harper-
 Trophy, 2001, 2002. (Series of three books about
 an ordinary girl who suddenly discovers that she's
 a princess of a small country.)

The Sisterhood of the Traveling Pants by Ann
 Brashares, Delacorte Press, 2001. (Well-loved story
 about a pair of pants and the three girls who wear
 them.)

Walk Two Moons by Sharon Creech, HarperTrophy,
 1996. (Touching, sometimes-sad story about a
 13-year-old girl whose parents have vanished.
 Recommended for preteens and younger teens.)

Divorce

Megann's Recommendations

Through My Eyes: A Journal for Teens by Linda Kranz,
 Rising Moon Publishers, 1998. (A journal with
 structure—you answer questions about goals,
 fears, family, dreams, opinions, and so on. You
 can just skip the questions that you're not sure
 about. This would be fun to look back on when
 you're older.)

Voices of Children of Divorce by David Royko, St.
 Martin's Griffin, 2000.

Website: allthelyrics.com (Find lyrics to your favorite songs. Megann puts them in her journal.)

CDs to drum to: *How I Do* by Res, MCA, 2001. (Really good pop artist—good voice, good songs, good beat.) *Solo Flight* by Corky Siegel, Gadfly Records, 1999. (Blues/rock—from her mom's collection but it really is a fun CD for drumming.)

Ali's Recommendation
How It Feels When Parents Divorce by Jill Krementz, Alfred Knopf, 1984. (Personal stories, as told by kids.)

Monique's Recommendation
Stepliving for Teens: Getting Along with Stepparents, Parents, and Siblings by Joel Block and Susan Bartell, Price, Stern, Sloane, 2001.

Insomnia

Julia's Recommendations
Relax and Renew: Restful Yoga For Stressful Times by Judith Lasater, Rodmell Press, 1995. (Good book for nighttime yoga poses, easy to understand.)

VHS or DVD: *Yoga Practice For Relaxation* with Patricia Walden and Rodney Yee. (One of the best yoga relaxation videos.)

Website: yogajournal.com (Lots of good info on yoga.)

Alice's Recommendations

Jazz CDs: *Come Away with Me* by Norah Jones, Blue Note, 2002. *The Look of Love* by Diana Krall, Verve, 2001.

Other Mellow CDs: *Acoustic Soul* by India.Arie, Motown, 2001. *A Day Without Rain* by Enya, Warner Bros., 2000.

Programs for downloading CDs onto your computer so that you can make mixes:
   Kazaa (kazaa.com)
   Limewire (limewire.com)
   Imesh (imesh.com)

Alice enjoys these poetry books as well:
Best-Loved Poems of Jacqueline Kennedy Onassis by
   Caroline Kennedy, Hyperion, 2001. (Many types
   of poems, from whimsical children's verse to
   classics.)
Chicken Soup for the Teenage Soul edited by Jack Can-
   field et. al, Health Communications, 1997, 2001,
   2002. (A series of three books that include inspirational stories and poems especially for teens.)
A Night Without Armor: Poems by Jewel Kilcher,
   Harper, 1999. (Personal, inspiring poetry by
   singer-songwriter Jewel.)

The Prophet by Kahlil Gibran, Knopf, 1993. (First published in 1923, this classic is a beautiful, poetic, spiritual story.)

Connie's Recommendation

Audiocassette/CD: *Art of Breath and Relaxation* by Rodney Yee. (Practical instruction on how to use your breath to relax. Find it online at yogajournal .com.)

Bullies

Anna's Recommendation

Women Who Run with the Wolves: Myths and Stories of the Wild Woman Archetype by Clarissa Pinkola Estes, Ballantine Books, 1992. (Stories and myths about strong, resourceful women.)

Laurie's Recommendation

DVD/VHS: *Miyazaki's Spirited Away*, Disney, 2002. (Animation feature film about a girl who inadvertently becomes the victim of intimidating "spirits"—and how she finds her own strength and courage to save herself and her parents. Not just a cartoon—it has won numerous awards, including the 2003 Oscar for best animated film.)

Lucinda's Recommendations

Letting Go of Anger: The 10 Most Common Anger Styles and What to Do About Them by Ron Potter-

Efron and Pat Potter-Efron, New Harbinger Publications, 1995. (Simple, effective strategies for dealing with your anger.)

Odd Girl Out: The Hidden Culture of Aggression in Girls by Rachel Simmons, Harcourt, Brace & Co., 2002. (Insight into how girls bully each other.)

Lesbian Teens

Lenni's Recommendations

Annie on My Mind by Nancy Garden, Farrar, Straus & Giroux, 1992.

To Believe in Women: What Lesbians Have Done For America—A History by Lillian Faderman, Houghton Mifflin Co., 2000.

Patience and Sarah by Isabel Miller, Fawcett Books, 1990.

Rubyfruit Jungle by Rita Mae Brown, Bantam Books, 1988. (Novel about a lesbian teen—a good, gritty story.)

Brenna's Recommendations

Is It a Choice? Answers to 300 of the Most Frequently Asked Questions About Gay and Lesbian People by Eric Marcus, HarperSanFrancisco, 1999.

Two Teenagers in Twenty: Writings by Gay and Lesbian Youth by Ann Heron, Alyson Books, 1995.

Helene's Recommendations

Free Your Mind: The Book for Gay, Lesbian and Bisexual Youth and Their Allies by Ellen Bass,

Perennial, 1996. (Really good practical advice on all sorts of issues.)

The Shared Heart: Portraits and Stories Celebrating Lesbian, Gay and Bisexual Young People by Adam Mastoon, HarperCollins, 2001.